D0699645

972.02
Ivanoff, Pierre
  Mayan enigma

72

001500   ch for a lost civ-
           rom the French by
    Elaine P. Halperin.   New York, Delacorte
    Press [c1971]
      202 p. illus. 22cm.

      Bibliography: p. 201-202.

      1. Mayas--Antiq.
    (Dept.)--Antiq.
    I. Title.
    [F1435.1P47I85

M
EL

MAYAN ENIGMA

THE SEARCH FOR A LOST CIVILIZATION

PIERRE IVANOFF

TRANSLATED FROM THE FRENCH BY
Elaine P. Halperin

DELACORTE PRESS / NEW YORK

CONTENTS

Eight pages of photographs follow page 104

PART ONE

PART
ONE

I

Introduction to the Mayan World

TWO frightened, screeching macaws fly away, spreading their splendid blue and gold plumage. A dark group of spider monkeys, their limbs frail, angrily toss dead branches and green fruit at me as they too fly off, screaming. I watch them as they go, my gaze lost in the tangle of huge trees in the wild forest.

More than one hundred feet above me the mad foliage of the tropics forms such a thick vaulted arch that the entire underbrush is bathed in twilight.

For the moment I have set aside my Western notion of nature's rhythm, where buds, flowers, fruit and dead leaves are so many stages marking the change of seasons. Here, in Petén, the vegetation always looks the same, even during the dry months. The foliage is unchanging, blossoming occurs at uneven intervals and the fruit ripens all year long. Some plants blossom only once in a life span.

The profusion of vegetation around me is bewildering. How can I pick out a particular aroma, a precise form, a spot of color in this mass of branches, so thick and overlapping that I cannot even identify a particular species? All I see above me is an immense roof of greenery.

3

Only the color and texture of the bark enables me to identify the immense trees that rise before me, as if to block my way. One species follows another. Thousands of plant parasites encrust the robust trees, ringing and enveloping them so completely that they hide them from view.

In this silent, suffocating foliage lianas predominate, followed by masses of orchids. These, proudly isolated, take root in stages, according to the species. The clusia fascinates me more than any of the other tree parasites. Its Spanish name, *matapalo* or "kill-tree," indicates its function. Oversized, like the giant it is, and strangling, it adapts itself to the form of the tree. When it can no longer do so, the orchid smothers the tree with its tentacular shoots which have become hopelessly encrusted.

Two acres of forest contain more than a hundred different scents, none of which are to be found in the neighboring acres. I must develop my sense of vertical vision in order to distinguish among the innumerable species that stretch upwards in impede my every step and that I constantly long to circum-search of the sun. And so these great trees, these obstacles that vent, become imposing giants with long, straight shafts. Their first branches appear very high up, about twenty-five feet above the ground, where the real drama is being enacted. Will the time ever come when I will be able to admire and touch the sumptuous, flamboyant bright orange flowers of the *Bernouilla flamea* which my companion, Rey, a great botanist, points out to me, uttering his laconic *"uacut"* and hitting the trunk with his machete?

In our difficult walk through this forest, I am second in line, leaving to one or the other of the three Indian guides who accompany me the task of clearing a path. An extended stay in this semi-obscurity, where one senses the presence of things but sees nothing precisely, will require retraining my hearing and my sense of smell. Each day, with every step I take, I learn something about the forest. I can now discern the animals that flee at our approach because I have learned how to identify instantaneously all the sounds that envelop us. Each daily incident, even the slightest, is a door that opens up a universe I am just beginning to understand.

For many years I have been attracted by this forbidding jungle, this kingdom of endemic diseases so typical of low altitude tropical countries. This is Petén. The size of Switzerland, it belongs to Guatemala.

In the Mayan language the word *petén* means "isolated places." In the extreme north of the region, in Yucatán, the word means "low plateau where woven baskets are suspended from the straw roofs of huts." The name is appropriate for this territory, which is isolated, inaccessible and very densely forested.

The peninsula of Yucatán, an arid land that belongs to Mexico, lies north of Petén. To the south the high plains of Guatemala separate it from the Pacific. On the west it is bordered by the Chiapas Mountains, on the east by British Honduras and the Republic of Honduras.

The yearning I felt for this country was not a romantic longing for the exotic but rather an urgent need for adventure and knowledge—the very same feeling that for the past fifteen years has sent me to the globe's most inaccessible tropical areas. It was certainly time to direct my energies to this region of Latin America, especially since my vocation as a traveler originated long ago when I discovered in the family library a large oldish album, illustrated with fine evocative engravings and entitled *Voyages d'exploration au Mexique et dans l'Amérique Centrale*. Written by Désiré Charnay, a great French traveler who lived during the middle of the last century, this fascinating book awakened in me an insatiable curiosity for distant lands and influenced all my adolescent reading. I devoured all kinds of books: Cook, Marco Polo, Bougainville, Pigafetta, etc. With great ease I moved from the discovery of the upper Nile to the discovery of Alaska. . . . I dreamt of becoming a Scott or a Livingstone.

I felt no apprehension whatsoever about embarking on this

Petén adventure. Exploration had been part of my life for so
long! How many experiences, sorrows and satisfactions the
forests of the New World had afforded me! Their naked
Indians attacked me, shouting and ordering me to dance;
Waïcan warriors, their faces painted, large bows in their
hands, captured me at Raudal des Gauharibos. But they paid
me the great honor of allowing me to discover the sources of
the Orinoco River. The equatorial forests of Asia acquainted
me with the unsullied cultures of the headhunters of Borneo,
the pygmoid tribes of Sumatra, the opium smokers of northern
Thailand. But they made me pay dearly for those fascinating
years: months of suffering in the hospital.

What surprises await me in the forests of Petén, that
setting for a grandiose self-revelation?

During the first millennium of our era the Mayans produced
the most resplendent Indian-American civilization of this continent.

Mathematicians of genius, astronomers, inventors of a
unique kind of writing, they knew nothing about metals. Their
tools were polished stones that so closely resembled those of
our Neolithic age that you might easily mistake them for such.
But they built sumptuous, sacred cities in the midst of this
virgin forest. In their imposing temples, perched on the summit of pyramids that in some instances rose 125 feet high,
ritual and initiatory ceremonies took place, to which a few
magnificently sculptured stones attest. Unfortunately, their
significance still eludes us. This is also true of Mayan hieroglyphics; experts have so far been unable to decipher most of
them.

What mysterious motives led the Mayan people to choose
the most inhospitable and most inaccessible region in all of
Central America as the place to fashion a superior civilization,
the most remarkable civilization on the new continent?

Another vexing question: the Mayans were the first to grow
corn; in fact, they were the first to pursue agriculture in
general. It was an essential foundation of their culture. But

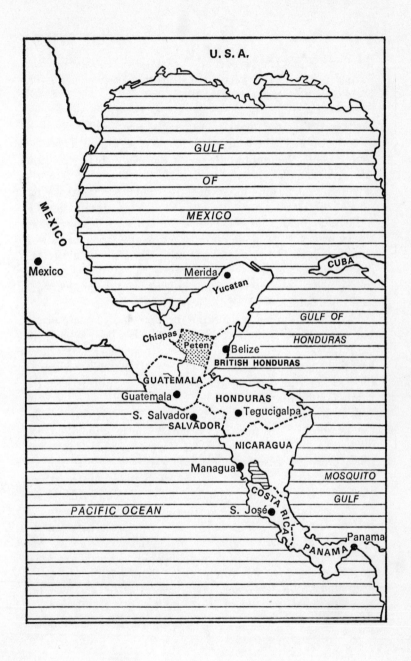

they never progressed beyond the stage of cultivating over
burned ground. They were satisfied to rely solely on a digging
stick which they also used as a dibble. Why?

The very origins of the Mayans are shrouded in mystery.
We know that the inhabitants of America arrived in small
ethnic groups. In the course of a lengthy migration that began
some twenty thousand years ago, they made their way from
Asia, crossing the Bering Straits. Did the Mayans follow the
same route? Did they figure in those shadowy migrations that
presumably traversed the straits much later, during the first
millennium before our era? Whence did they come, these short,
stocky men with aquiline noses, so unlike the other Indians of
America? J. E. Thompson, one of our great Mayan experts, has
observed that the Mayans may very well be distant cousins of
the Sumerian astronomers who built so many pyramids three
millennia before the Mayans appeared on the scene.

Physical anthropology informs us that, unlike their neighbors, the Mayans were and still are classified among the
world's most brachycephalic peoples. Their heart beats (fifty-
two per minute instead of seventy-two) approximate them to
the great mystics and masters of yoga who are able to slow the
rhythm of their hearts.

Actually, all the characteristics of the Mayans come under
the heading of the unusual. When a Mayan child died, the
mother would cut off one of her fingers and place it in the
tomb. Only the aristocrats were allowed to have hair on their
faces. Children's faces were therefore burned with scorching
cloths to make sure they would not later sprout beards. Cross-
eyes constituted the most prestigious of physical features. A
ball of resin tied to a strand of hair was hung between the
eyebrows of Mayan babies to make them cross-eyed. The
skulls of newborn infants were deliberately deformed in order
to obtain the high flat forehead so characteristic of Mayan
countenances in bas-reliefs. This last practice was also followed in the Near East and among the Incas.

But more bewildering than anything else is the fact that the

Mayan civilization inexplicably disappeared. During the tenth century A.D., several hundred years before the arrival of the Spaniards in America, the Mayans suddenly and for no apparent reason abandoned all their big stone cities to the encroaching forest.

For a long time it was thought that they had migrated to the north, to Yucatán, and toward the south, to Guatemala where their culture would have experienced a renaissance. The natives who today live in these two widely separated regions still employ the Mayan idiom. To be sure, throughout the entire classical period, which coincides with the era when Mayan civilization was in full bloom, both regions were centers of a flourishing culture. The most recent archeological studies, however, have demonstrated that this thesis is indefensible. The only incontrovertible statement we can make is that some definite relationship did exist between these regions.

But our question has not been answered. Why did these hundreds of thousands of highly civilized individuals suddenly disappear from Petén without leaving a trace? The enigma is all the more baffling because Petén, which today is deserted, had been the most densely populated area in Central America during the time when it was inhabited by the Mayans.

Attempting to solve the problem, I plunged into the voluminous literature on the Mayans. In Mexico I was fortunate enough to acquire for a very modest sum the books written by the earliest Spanish chroniclers and reissued by the local press. In New York I managed to obtain a popular edition of the books of Stephens, the father of Mayan archeology and the American counterpart of Désiré Charnay. Stephens was a talented writer and his famous book, *Incidents of Travel in Central America, Chiapas and Yucatán*, became a classic whose value was enhanced by the excellent drawings of his traveling companion, Catherwood. At Mérida, the capital of Yucatán, my basic library was enriched by a reissue of Landa's *Relación de las Cosas de Yucatán*, an indispensable work and the bible of all Mayanists. Forearmed by these

major sources, I read the works of such specialists as Maudslay, Spinden, Roys, Tozzer, Morley, Teeple, Thompson, etc.
The list is long.

I admired the objective observations of the archeologists,
the precision of their logic, the analytical quality of their
minds. But unfortunately the arguments advanced by some
were refuted by others. Endlessly I enumerated the many
contested hypotheses put forward to explain the disaster that
may have befallen the Mayans and caused them to flee Petén.
Here is a brief review of the principal ones.

Had a yellow fever epidemic occurred? History proves that
no contagious disease, not even the horrible plague, has ever
caused the fall of a civilization. Besides, why would such an
epidemic ravage only this region, leaving neighboring areas
unscathed? In any case, we now know that yellow fever was
introduced by the Spaniards.

Was there an earthquake? But in every part of the world
where earthquakes have occurred, large numbers of villages
continue to exist. Furthermore, there is no geological evidence
in Petén of any such occurrence; the ruins of the cities reveal
not a trace.

Did a drastic climatic change occur? No sign of it, answer
the dendrologists who have examined the rings in the tree
trunks of that period. Besides, specialists have demonstrated
that any unusual increase in rainfall would have helped agriculture, not hindered it. And a decrease in rainfall would have
changed nothing. The neighboring region of Yucatán, which
has no water course, provides living proof of this: here a half-
million Indians, who employ the same archaic methods of
cultivation used by the Mayans at Petén, continue to subsist.

Was there an agricultural disaster? It is altogether unlikely
that the soil gave out in Petén. Take, for example, the valley of
Motagua, the enclave of the traditional Mayans of Honduras.
Its soil has always been highly fertile, boasting such a wealth
of humus that tens of thousands of additional persons can live
off the land without exhausting it. Yet this is the region that
the Mayans first abandoned.

We are left, then, with the most logical hypothesis: an invasion by foreign barbarians such as occurred in the upper plains of central Mexico. But one essential fact demolishes this hypothesis: an invasion entails a large-scale occupation and usually generates a renaissance of the subjugated civilization. Nothing of the kind occurred in Petén. There is not the least archeological trace of a sudden flight from the land, of any deliberate destruction or of foreign occupation.

A few highly imaginative but scientifically rather unknowledgeable writers have suggested that the Mayans may have been perpetual nomads who were constantly tempted to venture off to new lands, and that each stage of their wanderings was marked by the erection of a large city. Unfortunately, an examination of the architectural styles of the old Mayan cities, to say nothing of the archeological evidence, explodes this otherwise very shrewd guess. All the cities of Petén sprang into being at approximately the same time and all were abandoned around the tenth century.

And so I reached an impasse, at least so far as bibliographical research was concerned. But instead of seeking a new interpretation of the archeological findings, I felt a growing conviction that some chance discovery would probably yield a clue to these cultural enigmas. As a matter of fact, I took very literally something J. E. Thompson had written on the subject: "We must not confine our search for the truth to those domains where we can be certain of finding it. If all scholars and students were to adopt such an attitude, there would be little chance of discovering the unknown, for success smiles only on those whose curiosity draws them far from the well-trodden paths."

Here was something that appealed to my own feelings! I was eager to seek the improbable. Perhaps the key to a solution of the problem was to be found among the two million Mayan-speaking Indians who still live in a tribal state on the upper plains of Guatemala. With this in mind, I spent an entire year with them, hoping to acquire a better understanding of what had occurred. It proved an enriching experience but opened no new vistas. And so the moment finally came to undertake an expedition into the jungles of Petén. Little did I suspect that I would make the most extraordinary of discoveries, one that would alter the entire course of my life.

II

On the Track of
Cortez' Horse

MY PREPARATIONS for departure had the quality
of a surrealist novel. Together with forest equipment, I took
everything a deep-sea diver would need. A minor but very
intriguing historical fact inspired my decision. I had discovered
in Guatemala's anthropological and historical library a book
authored by a seventeenth-century chronicler. Its story is well
worth telling.

In 1524 when the conquest of Mexico was nearing comple-
tion, Cortez, eager to reach Honduras, decided to traverse the
jungle of Petén. He chose the most difficult route. It would
have been far easier to go by sea.

The official purpose of the expedition was to take a certain
dissident captain, Cristobal de Ollid, by surprise and to punish
him. But that was probably just a pretext. Cortez, eternal
adventurer that he was, had always been fascinated by unknown lands. Tired of the political difficulties and administra-
tive problems deposited in his lap by his recent conquest, he
doubtless wanted to get as far away as possible from Mexico.

An enemy far more formidable than the Aztecs confronted
the Conquistador. He would have to move across impenetrable

marshy land, buried under a thick jungle, punctuated here and there by stagnant lagoons and dotted with wide, treacherous rivers.

The expedition lasted two years. Cortez' exhausting trek over more than fifteen hundred miles, five hundred of them covered with virgin forests, remains one of the greatest feats in the history of exploration.

He had 140 Spanish soldiers (including 93 cavalrymen), 3,000 Mexican Indians, 150 horses, 960 pigs, artillery, munitions and sundry provisions. The presence of large herds of pigs was quite usual in those times. They represented security in the form of tons of fresh meat: surely no one would die of hunger. Yet, despite all these precautions, the march through Petén proved horrifying, accomplished as it was by men who were starving. Chroniclers of the period cited definite instances of cannibalism in the Indian camp but said nothing about probable occurrences of the same kind among the Spaniards.

Cortez took with him on this mad venture Cuauhtemoc, an Aztec prince who had ascended the throne when his uncle, the Emperor Montezuma, was stoned to death by his own people for showing excessive servility toward the Spanish after the conquest. Hoping to give the Aztecs back their lost freedom, the young prince made a final effort to resume the armed struggle against the invader. His revolt came too late, and it proved futile. He was defeated. But he had shown himself to be so courageous that Cortez became his good friend. Relations between the two men were excellent.

However, from the very start of the Petén expedition, a succession of minor conspiracies within the army incensed Cortez. One day, without any proof of Cuauhtemoc's guilt, he accused the prince of high treason and had him hanged. The entire affair is still shrouded in mystery. History has never disclosed the reasons for Cortez' decision to take Cuauhtemoc on the expedition; it has likewise failed to reveal why he ordered the execution of his Aztec friend.

On March 13, 1525, after marching in a southeasterly direction, the exhausted army arrived at the banks of Lake Petén-Itzá in the heart of Petén. Taken by surprise, a few Indians who were fishing in the lake fled in their pirogues toward the isle of Tayasal in the center of the lake. But a large Spanish dog managed to catch hold of one of the men (all the stories about the conquest omit any mention of the important role played by these animals). Magnanimously, Cortez released the man and sent him back to his tribe, accompanied by a Spanish emissary who bore an invitation to King Canek.

On the following day a friendly meeting took place between the two chiefs. Canek, despite the isolation of his kingdom, knew all about Cortez, his conquest and his victories. Cortez was naturally amazed. The Itza tribe received him with great pomp, and this so pleased him that he decided to entrust his exhausted horse to Canek. Explaining that he would pick the animal up on his return, Cortez urged everyone to make sure that it was well cared for.

A horse at Tayasal! The Indians were overcome by this mark of trust. Like all the other inhabitants of the New World, they had never before seen a horse. This animal, which had galloped all over the American continent during prehistoric times, was gone by the time the first men appeared. It was the Spanish conquerors who reintroduced the horse to America. The horse had greatly facilitated the conquest of Mexico. Bearing a rider, it seemed to the Indians a powerful monster, a species of malevolent dragon, breathing fire and spreading death.

The Itzas manifested a genuine veneration for Cortez' horse. But unfortunately they knew nothing about feeding it. They treated the horse as a dignitary, offering it fermented drinks, spicy delicacies, turkey and other meats. Within a few weeks the poor beast died. The Indians feared the spirit of the dead horse quite as much as they dreaded possible reprisals when Cortez returned. Something had to be done. . . . The tribe's finest sculptors quickly went to work. In the main temple of the city a splendid stone horse soon came to occupy the place of honor. The Itzas called it *Tziminchac,* "god of thunder." They continued to make it innumerable offerings of flowers, pimento and corn alcohol. This time, of course, the horse ran no risk of suffering a fatal attack of indigestion.

Cortez never returned to Petén and thus never learned of the horse's fate. He arrived in Honduras in time to receive word that the rebellious officer he planned to punish had just been executed. His expedition had come to naught. He suffered an attack of malaria which left him totally exhausted. Taking advantage of his condition, Cortez' Spanish rivals ousted him and forced him to return to Spain. Shortly thereafter he died, victim of the aftermath of his last foolhardy venture in the New World.

For seventy years and despite several armies dispatched on three different occasions to fight against them, the Itzas refused to submit to the Spaniards. To be sure, the Spaniards had worn themselves out during the months-long march that brought them to the shore of Lake Petén-Itzá.

In 1618, after a long trip, two Franciscan missionaries, Father Orbita and Father Fuensalida, reached the banks of the lake. Such religious "shock troops" were often to be seen in New Spain. Usually they came alone, without escorts or weapons, to the most hidden and hostile regions where soldiers had often suffered severe defeats. Destined for the most part to perish on the natives' sacrificial altars, some of these shock troops occasionally succeeded in pacifying the Indian rebels. The role they played throughout the conflict was by no means negligible. Before embarking on such suicidal missions some priests said they hoped to die as martyrs; others, less fanatic, merely placed their fate in the hands of the good Lord, counting on his help to evangelize the natives and emerge from the adventure unscathed.

And so they went off, armed with their rosaries, their faith and a more or less thorough knowledge of the tribe they were to pacify and convert. Sometimes they were lucky enough to learn the language from prisoners or hostages.

For months, Father Orbita and Father Fuensalida had been trekking through the forest. In their desire to humble themselves, they walked barefoot! In a state of exhaustion, they finally reached the banks of the lake. Both men spoke fluent Itza (the Mayan-Yucatán language). They had just spent several years in Yucatán, spreading the good word in the language of the aborigines.

The Itzas, dumbfounded by the courage of these two strangers and beguiled by their words, which they naturally understood, welcomed them with all the honors generally accorded great tribal dignitaries. The priests were allowed to move about the country as freely as they wished.

After a few days' rest, Orbita and Fuensalida went to work. First, they systematically visited all the temples—twenty-one in all—to determine which idols the natives worshipped the most devoutly. They hoped thus to establish a logical sequence in their efforts to destroy the idols. At first the missionaries encountered nothing they had not anticipated. In Yucatán they had seen hundreds of such idols. But a shock was in store for them when they entered the principal temple and saw Tziminchac, proudly occupying the central position in the edifice. The Itzas were then worshipping a horse! What perversion! The Spanish chronicler, Villaguttiere, recounts that Father Orbita, filled with holy rage, flung himself upon the idol and tried to cast it down. This daring deed utterly bewildered the Indians.

Recovering quickly from their surprise, the Itzas dragged the two missionaries to the sacrificial altar. Father Fuensalida thought his final hour was at hand. He quickly launched into such inspired discourse that the Indians, diverted, forgot to massacre him. After many meetings and lengthy consultation, they finally decided to spare the missionaries provided they left Tayasal immediately, without a guide or any provisions.

The two Spaniards soon lost their way in the jungle. Exhausted and half-dead from starvation, they were lucky enough to happen on another Indian tribe, which rescued them.

The incident served as a warning to the Itzas. Clearly, the white man hated Tziminchac! In consequence their idol became all the more precious to them.

It was imperative to make sure that the statue of the horse was adequately protected. As soon as the missionaries had departed, the Indian priests loaded it onto a pirogue. They planned to hide it on a deserted shore of the lake where it would be safe from the inquisitive stares of other Spanish visitors. But the statue was very heavy. The Indian priests made one false move, whereupon the boat suddenly tipped to one side. The stone horse slipped overboard and disappeared forever in the dark waters of the lake.

But did it disappear forever? I was not so sure.

After carefully scrutinizing a number of Spanish works, I found that there were several different versions of the story. According to *Historia municipal del Reino de Yucatán,* the idol was made of wood, whereas Villaguttiere claimed that it was made of stone or lime (Could he have meant stucco?). Another account stated that the plaster horse had been broken by Father Orbita. The Itzas then supposedly ordered their sculptors to fashion a new stone Tziminchac. They were said to have carved it on the shores of the lake, at a place called Nic-Tun, a Mayan word meaning "stone point." Once the statue had been completed, so runs this version, it was transported by pirogue in the direction of Tayasal but never reached its destination because a violent storm overturned the pirogue.

In any event, all the details confirmed the fact that a statue of Cortez' horse had indeed existed. Moreover, it was very unlikely that the story about its disappearance was true. The idea of checking all this intrigued me. That is why I took deepsea diving equipment with me to Petén.

The descendants of the Itzas still live on an island in that lake, called Lake Flores today. They speak a little Spanish and have substituted shirts and pants for warriors' garb.

Oral tradition has it that the tribe settled here because of an unhappy love affair.

All the Itzas had left their native Yucatán a century before the arrival of Cortez. At that time the ambitious chief, Canek-ta, was in love with Sakonité, daughter of the king of Chichén-Itzá. Being of humble origin, he doubtless also hoped to consolidate his position by marrying the princess. But such presumption displeased the king, who decided to marry off his daughter to Prince Ulmil Itzahal. The importunate suitor was exiled to the distant abode of the people of Tocul. Enraged, Canek-ta kidnapped the young princess during the marriage ceremony. Realizing full well that he was risking a war of revenge, he decided to seek refuge in the heart of the Petén forest, and settled down on the shores of the island of Tayasal. Legend has it that the unhappy princess preferred death by drowning to yielding to her abductor. Years later her bones were found on the shores of the lake, near a beautiful white flower subsequently named *sak-nité* in memory of the girl. Ever since then this flower has been the symbol of purity and fidelity, the emblem of the province of Petén.

To match legend with historical fact, a red flower should have been added to symbolize all the blood spilled during the 170 years that followed Cortez' march through the territory; throughout this period the Spaniards' attempts to conquer the land were marred by one catastrophe after another.

Among these calamities were the two campaigns of 1623 and 1624, which took the lives of 250 Spaniards and enabled the Itza Indians to offer their idols the still palpitating hearts of white soldiers and Catholic priests.

In 1697 an army led by General Martin de Ursua reached the shores of Lake Flores. During the months-long march, the men endured terrible suffering. They finally settled in a place on the opposite shore of the island of Tayasal, despite the ominous sound of trumpets and war drums, the shrill tones of flutes and the volleys of arrows. In the space of twelve days, the Spanish carpenters doggedly managed to construct a small jail and a large pirogue. Anticipating some difficulties and hoping to arrive at a peaceful settlement, the Indians dispatched an emissary to parley with the invaders. But Ursua proved adamant and insisted on total surrender.

Having vainly tried every argument, the Indian chief filled four pirogues with the most beautiful women on the island and instructed them to divert and entertain the men in the Spanish encampment. What splendid ammunition! History does not reveal whether the women's mission was to wear the men out or merely to sow discord among them. Whatever their task, they failed completely.

On the morning of March 13, the Spaniards shoved aside the handsome Indian women and seized their boats. On the opposite bank, the Itzas, seated in light pirogues, peppered the enemy with volleys of arrows. Too impatient to wait until the light craft reached shore, the Spaniards jumped into the water. Then the real fight began. It was terrible and without mercy. Although it is only fair to say that General Ursua had categorically forbidden his men to use artillery or harquebuses, what ensued was a bloody massacre. Indeed, so frightful was the slaughter that the entire island population—women, children, old people, even the chiefs and warriors—went mad with fear and took to the water in the hope of escaping. Most of them drowned. The waters that ringed the island turned crimson with blood. Though weighted with heavy irons, even the Indian prisoners jumped into the water and perished in the lake.

After 170 years of struggle and failure, three hours of battle brought about the annihilation of the last bastion of Indian resistance to Spanish conquest. Of the eighty thousand members of the Itza nation, only a few scattered groups of fleeing Indians survived and they swore never to yield to the enemy.

From nine in the morning until five in the afternoon of the

following day, the victors were busy smashing all the idols in the huts and temples of Tayasal. To mark this great day with the traditional stamp of the Conquistador, General Ursua, accompanied by two priests, chose the site of the main temple as the place on which to build the new church. With great solemnity they put up a cross in front of the entrance. One note of irony: this was the very temple where, a century and a half earlier, the Itzas had erected the statue of Tziminchac, Cortez' horse! Inside the temple the three Spaniards noticed some bones dangling from the ends of colored ropes. Were these the venerated remains of the Conquistador's horse?

Tayasal, now a fief of the crown, proved to be a veritable inferno for the Spaniards. Completely isolated, decimated by disease, and lacking provisions, the invaders tried to obtain food by persecuting the neighboring Indians. The Indians retaliated by harassing the enemy at every turn. To be ordered to Petén soon became synonymous with being condemned to slow death. It was a way of punishing rebels and dissidents. This explains the stubborn refusal of many Guatemalans even today to give any information when the province of Petén is mentioned.

III

The First Clues

TO REACH Flores nowadays you have only to wait for favorable atmospheric conditions. An open field parallel to the lake serves as a landing site for small aircraft.

Consequently, I had no difficulty transporting my diving equipment: compressor, bottles, detonator, fuel, inflatable dinghy. Almost at once I found myself in a new world.

My equipment bewildered the inhabitants. It soon became apparent that my future underwater activities worried them as well. They never bathed in the lake. They were afraid of caimans—although these reptiles were scarce—and of small water tortoises with snakes' heads whose bite was poisonous. The people of Flores thought of the statue of Cortez' horse as a magically dangerous object whose image mysteriously appeared at times on the surface of the water only to disappear just as mysteriously. It was also rumored that Tziminchac was protected by a dragon.

I spent the first day diving but my efforts proved quite fruitless. The bottom of the lake was slimy and contained nothing but mud. This served to reinforce the Indians' conviction that the statue was magically protected. I myself was discouraged by the thought that Tziminchac must certainly be buried under many feet of slime. It was therefore pointless to continue searching in this place.

Out of sheer curiosity, I decided to extend my underwater explorations to other spots in the lake. Imagine the amazement of my audience when, on the following day and after two hours of searching, I brought to the surface, from a depth of one hundred feet, about ten pieces of centuries-old pottery! They were the color of lead—a characteristic feature of the artifacts of the pre-Columbian civilization of the Itzas. Presumably they had been thrown into the lake as an offering to the water gods.

From then on the Indians were persuaded that with my equipment anything was possible. They now regarded me as a genuine treasure hunter. I have frequently encountered the conviction that archeological research is merely a camouflaged treasure hunt. The aborigines show surprise at the interest archeologists display, for example, in terra cotta objects made centuries ago and to which they ascribe no value whatsoever. Often they break them in the hope of finding hidden gold or precious stones, a possibility that seems likely to them in view of the foreigners' eagerness to find such objects.

I tossed the pieces of pottery back into the lake to prevent their being needlessly destroyed. The Itzas placed a strange interpretation on my action. They surmised that if I was so indifferent to these ancient earthenware receptacles, it must be because I was looking for Montezuma's treasure.

The suspicion that part of the treasure of the last Aztec emperor was hidden in Petén was widespread among the Indians of northeastern Guatemala. It was thus that they explained both Cortez' foolhardy expedition to their land and the failure of Cuauhtemoc's conspiracy. Cuauhtemoc had presumably tried to prevent Cortez from recovering the treasure. It was assumed that the Conquistador took his royal prisoner along on the expedition in order to extract information about the famous treasure.

An obscure affair that occurred during the last century seemed to confirm suspicions about the location of the treasure. In 1846 a group of Indians from Petén settled in a village in British Honduras, between Petén and Yucatán. They claimed to have fled a war forced upon them by a neighboring tribe. Three months after their arrival, they burned and pillaged the village. Then they fled back to their native land. A reconnaissance patrol sent in pursuit caught up with them four days later near the lagoon of Yaloch. The Indians offered a curious bargain to the twenty-five half-breed soldiers and their commanding officer, a native of Italy. They would leave their families behind as hostages for a space of eight days, the time necessary to search for the gold that would buy back their freedom. The bargain was concluded. One week later the Indians returned, bringing with them twenty-six bars of gold in the shape of cylinders, engraved with hieroglyphics and drawings of eagles' crests. This was Emperor Montezuma's seal!

I was growing weary of these sterile suppositions and tall tales. But I pricked up my ears when four Indians swore to me that the treasure of their ancestors lay at the bottom of the flooded grottoes surrounding the distant lake of Petexbatun, a sacred body of water. I had explored endless caves during my years on the lofty plains of Guatemala. I had often discovered archeological relics and occasionally very recent signs of witchcraft séances. There was not the slightest doubt in my mind that the great Mayans of the classical era had had a genuine grotto cult. I was therefore quite pleased with the new itinerary that had just been spontaneously suggested to me. It suited my inclination to penetrate a little deeper into the Mayan jungle which I wanted so much to explore.

It took me no time at all to dispose of some of my bags and to organize a small expedition which, after a few days' trek, brought me to a tributary of the Rio de la Pasión. From there, with an Indian guide named Eusebio, a three-day journey by pirogue brought me to the lake of Petexbatun.

Once again I realized that so powerful is the imagination of these people that they lose sight of reality. In this wild magnificent country the lake certainly has something magical about it, but I saw no sign of a grotto. The somberness of the waters and the presence of a few caimans soon put an end to my deep-sea diving. But I was happy to prolong the trip, methodically exploring the shores of the lake, the narrow water courses that flowed into it and the marshy stretches all around.

It was then that my pirogue came upon a trapper, fishing. It was a perfect time for this. During the dry season the river literally swarms with life. Parched animals come to the banks to drink. The water line is lower and this makes it more transparent. Innumerable schools of fish come and go in search of food. It is a most difficult time for fish, very different from the rainy season when violent currents separate bits of earth from the wooded banks and thus bring fruits, insects and worms into the water. Now, during the dry season, the river's current is scarcely perceptible. In the deeper pockets the waters are dormant. They are also so warm that the fish constantly surface to breathe in a little air.

"Crocodile fish" abound in the lake of the Petexbatun. Immobile, they float on top of the water and are so easily approached that I managed to kill three of them with a machete. Their firm white flesh is delicious and curiously like that of the crocodile they resemble.

The solitary woodsman had set up camp in a gay, sunny spot on the shores of the lake. The fish he had caught during the last few days were hung up to dry. At nightfall he had merely to walk a few yards to lay down his lines along the bottom of the lake where schools of fish swam about. At dawn he would raise the lines with a look of obvious satisfaction. He knew every rock, marsh and stream in or around the lake. Every day, seated in his pirogue, he would cover dozens of miles of his kingdom.

I immediately dubbed him "the Man of the Petexbatun," the

very name I myself was later to be given in Guatemala. After some initial hesitation, he agreed to teach me his fishing techniques. Soon he took me with him everywhere, while Eusebio, my placid guide, settled down in the camp like a king and supervised the drying of the fish. Occasionally Eusebio would go off to hunt. He had a predilection for iguanas, those giant lizards that look positively antediluvian. They cling in clusters to the branches of trees that overhang the lake. The least alarm send them diving from a great height into the dark waters. Eusebio would watch them for hours at a time, waiting for the moment when one of them would jump toward the shore. Then he would bear down on it with a sure hand. He cooked it with great care, either roasting or boiling it as the mood took him.

The fishing tackle the Man of the Petexbatun used most frequently was a bamboo harpoon about four and a half yards long. In our expeditions my role usually consisted of silently steering the pirogue as close as possible to the schools of fish. Then I would watch him go into action, and it was marvelous to behold. At first I had some difficulty maneuvering the pirogue because I was unaccustomed to the long oar with a narrow blade that the people of Petén use in place of the usual paddle. You have to stand up in the boat, and this makes for instability. But experience has proved to my satisfaction that this kind of oar is exactly the right shape for use in this country. In the shallows it serves as a perch; in the marshy stretches you use it as a pole to propel the pirogue forward, something practically impossible to do with a paddle. It can also be used as a harpoon to capture tortoises. When Lisandro, as the Man of the Petexbatun is called, explained this to me, I expressed such skepticism that he immediately gave me a demonstration.

We were paddling down the Petexbatun River as it courses from the lake to Rio de la Pasión, which is a large tributary of the Usumacinta. The tortoises like this place. But that day they were particularly distrustful and refused to put in an appearance. Thereupon Lisandro began to whip the water violently with his oar, as if he wanted to punish the river. He asked me to do the same. I did.

"The tortoises will be afraid," he told me. "They'll seek a hiding place along the banks, on top of the water. . . . Look!"

And indeed, I soon spotted two dark masses flattened on a muddy shore along the right bank. Silently, Lisandro gestured to me to steer the pirogue toward the larger one. In a flash he plunged a long pointed piece of metal into the tortoise. This pointed metal was tied to a string which in turn was fastened to the oar through a little hole which had hitherto intrigued me. Lisandro threw his oar as you would hurl a projectile. Taken by surprise, the tortoise tried to flee. The pointed piece of metal, imbedded in the carapace, was suddenly detached from the oar. Nevertheless, the poor tortoise could not escape. It was not strong enough to pull the heavy wooden oar. Lisandro bent over quickly, picked up the tortoise, which was thrashing about helplessly, and deposited it in a corner of the pirogue.

Freshwater tortoises represent precious reserves of fresh meat for woodsmen. The capacity of these animals to survive is quite extraordinary. For weeks at a time they can remain absolutely immobile with no food whatsoever and seem none the worse for it.

Within the waters, the principal enemy was the caiman. Its cry is like the croak of the grasshopper and Lisandro could imitate it perfectly. This enabled him to locate the caiman in its hole and to bar its way by placing a solid barricade of hard wood in front of the opening. So convinced was he of the danger of these reptiles that I no longer had any desire to swim in the lake, which thus far I had been doing without incident for the sheer pleasure of it.

Then, one morning, as we rounded the bend of the Petex-batun, we surprised two magnificent tortoises lying on top of the water. As we approached, they quickly dived to the lake's bottom. Before Lisandro could attach the metal point to his

harpoon, they were beyond reach. The water, clear as always
in this spot, was less than fifteen feet deep. Without further
ado, I dived after them and caught one of the fugitives
without too much difficulty, although it struggled desperately.
It was a fine specimen, weighing more than twenty pounds.
Lisandro was amazed. Not only had I dived into the water but
my fishing technique had proved as effective as his own. I
must admit that I was just as surprised as he. After that my
skill improved so much that the very sight of all the tortoise
dishes we had to eat began to sicken me.

When I first began accompanying Lisandro, our relationship
was rather curious. He said little and seemed disinclined to
want company. The diving equipment I had unloaded on his
camping ground intrigued him but he hardly took my underwater explorations seriously. In his view, as in that of all
woodsmen, what I was doing amounted to sheer folly.

From the time I caught the tortoise Lisandro's attitude
toward me changed. He was more trusting and friendly. Soon
he told me that the grottoes that supposedly ringed the lake
were pure figments of the imagination. But, he said, he knew
of a real cave in the heart of the forest, where a small
underground river ran.

"For someone like you it isn't dangerous, and maybe you'll
find a treasure," he said seriously. Then he added quickly,
"Half of it for me, okay?"

How could he ever be made to understand that a few
fragments of good pottery would seem to me the finest of
treasures? What could I hope to find in the midst of this wild
forest of Petexbatun, as yet largely unexplored and devoid of
archeological interest?

And yet . . . The very next day there I was, my bag slung
over my shoulder, trudging with Lisandro in the huge forest.
The placid Eusebio had decided not to accompany me and
was staying in camp.

Two days of fairly easy walking brought us to a rather vast
cave which my companion let me enter alone. He was afraid
of the spirits.

All I had in the way of equipment was an ordinary flashlight, which obliged me to swim with my right hand held up in the air. It was rather unpleasant because the river was quite cold, although not very deep. I had been swimming no more than ten minutes when I realized I was wasting my time. There was nothing in the back of the cavern but rocks, earth and thousands of terrified bats that dashed against my flashlight and my face.

Disappointed and shivering with cold, I was delighted to return to the stifling heat of the forest and the vexed expression on the face of my companion.

It was then that I made an amazing discovery. It restored my faith in my own imagination just when I was feeling so deflated. For many years to come, the entire course of my life was to be completely transformed by this discovery. I was bending down to replace my flashlight in the pocket of my bag. Right there, at my feet, I suddenly noticed two fragments of pottery. They were not extraordinary, of course, but I was nevertheless moved by the sight of these curved, terra cotta potsherds. I held them in the hollow of my hand and showed them to Lisandro, my heart pounding. My companion made a face.

"You can find that kind of junk everywhere around here."

Then I looked around. I realized that I was standing directly in front of a hillock, uniformly rounded, not very high, and covered with vegetation.

What was this? A trick of nature? I was suddenly convinced that the mound was definitely archeological in origin. What ancient constructions was it concealing—here, in the midst of a virgin forest, far from the river? To be sure, many large Mayan cities had been discovered in Petén during the early years of the twentieth century. But they are hundreds of miles from here. Everyone said that the region of Petexbatun had always been deserted. Well, then?

Feverishly, I dug into the soil in search of more significant archeological relics, such as the remains of buildings. But in vain. Close to the cave I found a few more fragments which confirmed my feeling that the first ones I had found had not been lying there by accident.

How could I fail to believe in all that these fragments and the strange mound seemed to promise? Surely they would interest amateurs of archeology in Guatemala. I had only one thought: to tell people there about the existence of these promising clues.

Upon my return to Guatemala, I met with only indifference, sarcasm or suspicion. People said to me: "We don't know Petexbatun at all." "Are you sure you really went to Petén?" "How much did you pay for those potsherds?" "Petexbatun? But see here, that's a place where nobody has found anything."

Disappointed and somewhat perplexed by such indifference to my fragments of pottery, I decided to return and find more convincing evidence. That is why I am now leading the precarious life of a woodsman, in the company of three *chicleros*—"hunters of chicle gum."

IV

Exploration Techniques

VAMPIRES! Vampires!" Rey shrieks.

He pulls the machete from its sheath and cuts down two slender branches. He tosses one to me while a cloud of slowly moving winged mammals descends on our camp.

Julio and Lisandro also cut two branches for themselves. Rey makes me sit down back-to-back with him and side-by-side with the other two. The four of us form a compact group. The muffled sound of the blood-sucking vampire bats, their wings grazing us as they pass, is rather frightening. I lower my head, hunch up my shoulders and imitate my companions. They have anchored the pliable branches between their knees, using them to fan away the vampires. This newly discovered weapon is the only protection we have against the onslaught of the bats.

They have probably been attracted by the small clearing we have made for our camp tonight rather than by our mere presence or the hope of a good meal at our expense. But I am not entirely reassured. Nothing is more impressive than these mammals that band together to attack you, emitting low shrill cries.

Our waving branches turn the trick! After a few minutes the vampire bats fall to the ground by the dozens, but most of them fly away.

A few days before we probably would have laughed at the incident. But tonight everything seems to conspire against us, and we are possessed by a vague sense of anxiety. My usually hardy chicleros are nervous and irritable. So am I.

Since yesterday all of nature seems to have become hostile to us. We are in bad humor and the least little thing is magnified into a catastrophe. It's probably fatigue. Ten weeks ago we dried out our pirogue and covered it with branches. Then we set out, advancing each day ever deeper into the forest. These have been ten weeks of alternating hope and disappointment, ten weeks in which so many difficulties have arisen that we all have the feeling that the end of our adventure is at hand.

Actually, the first heavy rainfalls are the major cause of our weariness. Not only have they destroyed our morale, they also make us more vulnerable to attacks of malaria or dysentery. It seems as if the number of insects that constantly harass us has quadrupled in the last three days. We are floundering in mud and our clothes reek of dampness.

Neither the pumas, the jaguars nor the vampire bats present any real danger. Our true enemies are the parasites and mosquitoes. The insects that are rampant in daytime miraculously disappear ten minutes before nightfall. Then fresh waves of insects of all kinds replace them. Even their sting or bite is different. The mosquito nets offer no protection; the insects are so tiny that they slip through the mesh. Their bite feels like a slight burn.

For the last three days even the ticks have become unbearable. And yet we should be used to living with these parasites that infest the underbrush and swarm over unhappy travelers. So voracious are they that, given enough time, they can increase to ten times their normal size. If you remove a tick from your skin too roughly, its head remains imbedded in your flesh and can cause an infection.

But in my opinion the most virulent parasite is the *col-moyote*. It penetrates the skin and then begins to expand in its soft refuge. You have to wait about three or four days, until it grows quite large. Only then can you remove it. It's a difficult operation if you are at all squeamish. You have to place a lit cigarette close to the area where it has burrowed. Then it's a matter of enduring the pain of the singed flesh until the intruder has been overcome. When the insect's head emerges, you burn it immediately with cigarette ash. Then you remove the entire animal. This hurts because by then it has grown to the size of a chick-pea.

I have noticed to my sorrow that the colmoyote prefers my European flesh to that of my companions. Can it be that the Indian race is immune? The correct explanation is probably that I take advantage of every chance I have to go swimming whereas the chicleros never come in contact with water except to drink it. Nothing in the world can make them remove their shirts to wash. But they drink the most polluted water with the greatest of pleasure and suffer no ill effects, whereas one sip of it is enough to upset me for the entire day. I therefore try whenever possible to quench my thirst with moisture obtained from lianas.

Last week, large black flies created a panic in our camp. As soon as they appeared, Rey, Lisandro and Julio, without exchanging a word, hurriedly dug a hole in the ground to bury our supplies of meat, which were wrapped in palm leaves. A single fly of this species lays hundreds of eggs, even on meat as it is being roasted on a grill. Within a few seconds the eggs hatch and swarms of crawling maggots appear.

But the worst of the lot is a smaller fly which we spotted for the first time this morning, the *mosca chiclera*. It is a carrier of the protozoa of leishmaniasis which causes the skin to fester, especially the cartilaginous areas of the face—the nose and ears. A few German laboratories have just perfected a very expensive remedy for leishmaniasis. If used carefully and in time, it occasionally halts ulceration. The chicleros, for their part, resort to a drastic remedy. They smear the affected area with a thick layer of rubber derived from the rubber plant. Within a few days the air hardens this latex solution, which thus tightens over the ulcerated area. Then this home-made plaster covering is brutally ripped off, and off too come the diseased areas of the skin. The process is both radical and painful and often results in serious disfigurement. But it is preferable to the frightful skin ulcerations that cause an incessant itching that is maddening. Anyone unfortunate enough to suffer from leishmaniasis of the throat, a malady that luckily is quite rare, is sure to die of it.

The three tough and taciturn men who accompany me belong to that new breed of forest adventurers, the chicle hunters. Chicle, which is indispensable for the manufacture of chewing gum, comes from the sap of a huge wild tree known as the sapodilla. It is prevalent in Petén. The life style of these chicleros, as well as the methods they use to obtain sap from the tree trunks, is similar in every way to those of the Brazilian *seringueiros* in the Amazons.

Mayan archeology owes a great deal to the chicleros be-cause their ventures in the forest led to the discovery of most of the ancient cities.

I know that my three companions are here to forget their past and that it would be most unhealthy, to say the least, to question them on the subject. Our life in common, however, has given me a few clues.

All three have Spanish first names. Rey, however, is a pure Quiché Indian who escaped from a coffee plantation on the high plains of Guatemala where he had been treated as a slave.

Lisandro is a mulatto, a descendant of the Black Africans who today are a major part of the population of British Honduras.

As for Julio, he is the offspring of a Lecandon Indian father and an Itza mother.

These men are permanent residents of Petén. What a curious fate has befallen this mysterious region, reduced to virtual oblivion ever since the Mayans of the classical empire disappeared! Nowadays it is occupied by a few hundred individuals who have come from elsewhere.

The nature and mentality of the chicleros remind one of the gold and diamond seekers from South America, among whom I lived for so long. Perhaps that is why I feel entirely at home with these men. They are brave but superstitious, demanding yet generous. It is not easy to obtain their help, even if you pay them well. But once they agree to join you, they are just as tenacious as you are in pursuing any common undertaking.

Since we all approved of one another after a few brief expeditions, the three men readily agreed to accompany me on this adventure.

I carry on such lengthy monologues with myself during our long daily treks that I manage to forget for a while the heavy responsibilities I have incurred as well as the mosquitoes that are constantly assaulting my hands and face. I can't help smiling when I think of the conventional image of the old-time explorer with his helmet and boots. I wear basket-weave shoes. They are light and not very sturdy, but they never cause blisters and they shed water as easily as they take it in. The buttons on my shirt sleeves have all popped, so I bind my cuffs to my wrists with very thin strands of liana—anything to prevent the mosquitoes from biting. I've tried every possible remedy against mosquito bites—special preparations, lemon, soap, mud. Nothing works. Besides, in the space of a few minutes, my sweat washes it all away. No one uses headgear anymore. You wouldn't be able to stand it in this oven where the body is always dripping with sweat. The perspiration on my forehead keeps running into my eyes and irritating them. This disturbs my vision.

A string of tree bark dangles like a long necklace on my chest. The ends are tied together at the top of the bag on my back. This serves as a belt of sorts that I slide over my forehead from time to time and which I pull with both hands at ear level. It's an old trick I learned from the trappers of

South America, a way of easing the load on your back. The effort produces a real feeling of relief.

I tie my machete in its leather sheath to one side of my bag because I can never get used to the way it swings back and forth against my right thigh. Should I need it I can reach it with a flick of the hand.

I try to resist the reverie that isolates me momentarily from the outside world. I envy my Indian companions their capacity to remain alert at all times. They are so perfectly adjusted to this difficult milieu that they don't seem to tire. You never see a drop of sweat on their impassive faces, even when they have to make the most strenuous efforts. These men are capable of chasing game after several hours of march without even bothering to deposit their bags.

Naturally, we all eat the same food. Yet for these men the diet seems better suited to the precarious life we lead. For example, tonight they will consume three times more of the Mexican hog known as peccary than I will. And they will digest it perfectly! Tomorrow they will walk effortlessly until evening without stopping once to eat, whereas this obligatory diet will give me real stomach pains. When we started off, the most difficult thing for my companions was to give up corn, their basic and habitual source of nourishment. We couldn't take any along because corn can be eaten only after lengthy preparation. Besides it does not expand when cooked. Hence I preferred to take non-decorticated rice with us. It is more nutritious than corn, cooks faster and quintuples in volume.

Each of us carries the same amount of weight in our shoulder bags. When we started off our provisions included rice, coffee, salt, sugar, grease, a little tea. We reduced to a minimum any additional equipment such as bedding, cameras, cooking utensils, ammunition, fresh clothes, batteries, etc. Nonetheless, at the outset our bags each weighed almost ninety pounds.

What curious work it is to look for ruins! Not only do you have to carry a heavy load; you also have to walk for days and weeks, eat as little as possible in order to conserve supplies and always leave a trail behind you with your machetes in case you get lost and should have to find your way back. The process is exhausting, but it has the advantage of enabling you to explore in the space of two months a territory that a conventionally equipped but less mobile expedition, with a large number of porters, would take six months to cover. I must add that in Petén you have to move quickly because you can cover a great deal of ground only during the dry season, a period of four months at the most. As soon as the rains come, the entire region is transformed into a gigantic swamp.

We knew when we left that our provisions would not last for more than three weeks. One general rule is accepted by all seasoned trappers and I myself have verified it more than once: no matter how strong a man may be, he cannot carry on his back provisions for more than twenty days. If he attempts to carry more, he will eat more; in the end he will realize that his self-sufficiency will last no longer than the usual three weeks.

We were able to hold out for more than two months only because we hunted. Knowing that we would hunt, I had tripled the amount of salt we took along. It is absolutely necessary to put salt on everything you eat in this country because dehydration is a constant factor.

As for the problem of water, it is solved by the presence of lianas. They slow us up at every step but they are welcome when a halt is called. Veritable reservoirs of drinking water, the lianas are our allies during the time of year when water spots everywhere are completely dried up.

My companions taught me to pick out those lianas whose stalks contain the best drinking water. There is one species with a very bitter sap, the color of licorice; this is the liquid we have been drinking for the past few days in place of our morning coffee. To make the best possible use of it, you have to cut the liana quickly from a stalk about a yard long. If you cut too slowly, the sap will rise and ooze out of the stump.

Rey, for his part, prefers the silk-cotton trees (*bombax*) which contain considerable reserves of water whose taste, he claims, is unequaled.

By now I have learned to recognize the abundant fauna of the forest: the waggish kinkajous, the prehistoric-looking armadillos, the long-nosed tapirs, the agoutis with their fatty flesh. All these animals have become familiar to me.

Such recognition is ordinarily associated with our gastronomical experiences; most of our meals consist of a variety of birds: parrots, toucans, red-breasted *couroucous,* humming birds—which, because they slow their heartbeats at night can easily be caught without even being awakened; delicious *hoccos,* woodland partridge.

The forest trembles with torrential rains. Lisandro, who is in the lead, stops and turns, puzzled by a sound that seems to grow louder and draw nearer. A frightful odor accompanies this furious rumbling. Peccaries! We scarcely have time to move aside before a horde of Mexican hogs, their heads lowered, lunge in our direction. We can tell by their looks that they are in a dangerous mood.

Swiftly, Lisandro seizes his old twenty-two rifle, a very practical weapon because both it and its shells are light. To use it successfully you have to be a very good shot indeed, but the abundance of unwary wild game simplifies the problem. It seems impossible, however, to fire on this horde of animals. No one would survive the charge of a hundred enraged peccaries. Rumor has it that Mexican hogs are capable of spending days tearing up the ground to uproot trees where imprudent hunters have sought refuge. If we want to replenish our meat supply we would do better to wait for a straggler. Hastily, we seek safety behind a thick tree and wait motionlessly for the laggards frisking about in small groups.

Lisandro is a crack shot. Like his companions, he has a great respect for wild game. This is something I fully appreciate. Here it is perfectly senseless to kill for the sake of killing. Our way of hunting, which is characteristic of all trappers, would shock conventional sportsmen. Usually we come as close as possible to the animals and wait until they have stopped moving. Now, Lisandro aims at a lone peccary and pulls the trigger. But the gun is jammed and doesn't go off. Unfortunately, this kind of thing happens quite often. Our guns are old and not well cared for; the shells are of poor quality, having been sold by trappers who had originally purchased them at a discount.

Apparently we will have to forego meat for our evening meal. But suddenly Julio rushes forward, shouting at us to follow him with our machetes. Hard on his heels, I crash into a heavy male peccary that runs off quickly. Two more peccaries lunge forward; unaware of my presence, they ram into me as they pass. I lose my balance and grab at a palm tree to steady myself; it is covered with prickles. Furious, I rush in pursuit of the peccaries and like a fool trip over a tangle of lianas. My Indian companions seem to have their hands full, too. The blades of their machetes merely graze the beasts and inflict no wounds. And now the entire herd has gone by, even the stragglers, and here we are, furious, feeling foolish. No luck! But, wait a minute. . . . Rey has just spotted a lone straggler, the very last and a good-sized one at that. Suddenly, Rey begins to bark like an angry dog. Julio follows suit. Startled, the peccary hesitates, panics, circling around and around. Joining the general uproar, I begin to bark too. We sound like prehistoric men. Very cautiously, we encircle the animal. He finally squats down, baring his teeth. In one leap, Julio flings himself on the beast and kills it with his machete.

There it is, our peccary, hanging from a tree like a quartered beef in a butcher's shop. Its front paws are bound by two strands of liana. Very carefully, Lisandro removes the musk gland from the lower spine. It discharges such an overpowering odor that the forest still reeks of it twenty-four hours later. We build a bonfire in order to burn all the animal hair and kill every single tick that might be lodged there. We want to make sure that none survive. We already harbor enough of them.

Lisandro quickly slices up the meat and packs huge slabs of it in leaves. We tie these securely to our bags with thin strips of liana. Then we resume our march.

We always halt for two hours toward the end of the afternoon, before sunset, to set up camp for the night. We leave at dawn the next day.

Certain things determine our choice of site: first, the proximity of water; second, the presence of palm trees, which we need for the construction of our temporary shelters. Already the rains are beating down on the forest and we sorely need a roof over our hammocks. Besides, each of us wants to feel protected and isolated from all that lives and moves atop the vast cupola of foliage.

Isn't it true that we are intruders in this forest? The sapajous, those large, shrieking monkeys, certainly seem to think so. They are scandalized by the way we make ourselves at home. During the day they merely observe us from their perch in the trees. But when night falls and we are asleep, they regale us with a concert of sinister shrieks that awaken us with a start. Poor sapajous! All they can do is frighten people. They are otherwise quite harmless. Their sedentary nature has proved their undoing. Always congregated in groups in the same places, they are literally being decimated by yellow fever.

In order to pitch camp quickly, each of us has his own special task to perform. Rey and I clear the site with our machetes, an indispensable tool without which the trapper cannot survive. Lisandro and Julio lop off huge leaves from the palm trees. Our shelter is fashioned according to the species of palm trees we happen upon. The guana requires a pole to support the leaves that fall at angles and cover the sides. Tonight the corozo palm will shelter us. We build a kind of hooded hut for each of us, covered with huge leaves spread out like a fan. We drive stakes tied with flexible, strong strips of liana, which we also use to attach our hammocks high enough so that we won't have any contact with the earth and its swarming life.

Julio is busy doing what he does each day and is expert at: concocting a grill on which to cook our meat. He places it approximately two feet above the ground. It serves in lieu of a food locker. The flames of the fire will preserve the meat through the night. By morning the entire outer surface will be burned to a crisp. We can preserve our meat supply for about ten days if we remember each night to place it on the grill. This is the technique used in smoking meat. Many American Indians still smoke their game on grills that exactly resemble Julio's. The method is quite ingenious and can be used for animals that have not been stripped of their skin or fur. Actually, the meat tastes all the better for having been smoked in this way. The only drawback is that you have to get up several times during the night to stoke the fire. But this doesn't seem to bother Julio.

Once again the ingenuity of my companions, coupled with nature's abundance and generosity, will guarantee me a good night's camping. Unfortunately, my momentary sense of well-being is not enough. In view of the circumstances, especially with the rainy season about to begin, I doubt whether we'll be able to hold out much longer.

Squatting a few feet away from the fire, in the thick smoke that for the moment protects me from mosquitoes, I watch the three men who during the past two months have been working miracles to solve our food problem.

Am I on the eve of defeat? Judging by the sites of the various mounds we discovered in the course of these last weeks of exploration, the answer is probably yes. Not once did we find a single sculptured relic in the vicinity. And yet the region must once have been inhabited. Both the mounds and the fragments of pottery attest to this.

But my conviction that the area is archeologically important can only be confirmed by the discovery of tangible architectural remains or sculptured stones at a particular site.

In the course of our wanderings we have discovered numerous sites dotted with artificial mounds; but these will convince no one. Even the rather curious, evenly shaped,

pointed hill which should, in my opinion, be reason enough for
a mission, will not arouse any interest. The hill is so large and
the surrounding forest so dense that I have abandoned the
idea of photographing it.

Where are the ancient Mayan temples and cities hidden?
Will these two months of searching lead to nothing? And yet
the site at which we have just set up camp seems promising.
. . . An intuition? Perhaps. But in a venture such as this, can
common sense really prove useful?

V

The Discovery of a City

FOR three days we continue our feverish search. We blaze trails to be used as landmarks and humanize this small section of the virgin forest. We clear an extensive area around the four hills covered with dense vegetation and topped by giant trees. Once again I tell myself repeatedly and with conviction that these hills are man-made, that they conceal something, that people once lived here.

In this spot the mounds are far more numerous than elsewhere. Their height, from 15 to 115 feet, their perfectly rounded forms, their unexpected presence, their proximity to one another—everything seems to suggest that this is a fairly important archeological site. And yet there's not a single clue, not even a small piece of sculptured stone. Among the tangles of roots there is naught but pebbles and rich soil. A final probing yields nothing.

Nonetheless, the small territory exists, though its clues are few. The vegetation is denser here and the fauna abundant. This can be easily explained. The Mayans strewed and ringed their sacred cities with rare trees and fine fruits. After they abandoned the cities, their carefully selected species proliferated, crowding out other wild species. Thereafter these choice trees constituted a veritable orchard in the heart of the forest.

The sapodilla tree (*Achras zapota*) was the first to be selected by these perceptive Mayans. It was chosen in part because of its chicle sap, which people chewed even then. But the main reason was the fine quality of its hard, durable wood, which was used for construction as well as for major masonry. The single important wooden inscription dating from the classical Mayan period occurs on a lintel from Tikal; carved from the bark of a sapodilla tree, it can be admired today at the ethnographic museum in Basel, Switzerland. Even today, in the ancient temples of Yucatán and Petén, we find beams made of sapodilla wood that for over a thousand years have separated the overhanging arched walls from the chambers inside. It is true, of course, that the construction of these overhanging walls is so specially contrived as to prevent pressure from being exerted on the wood.

This tree is also valued for its fruit, the naseberry. We could feast on it often if only the monkeys didn't like it so much. They hardly wait for the fruit to ripen. So greedy are they that they usually bite into it when it is still green, only to throw it away in disgust because of its sour taste. We often see unripe naseberries on the ground. Sooner or later the peccaries will eat them.

It is thus plain that the presence of sapodillas indicates the proximity of monkeys. And wherever sapodilla trees grow in abundance, ruins are very likely to be found. This is an almost invariably verifiable observation. But I say nothing about this to my companions. They are, therefore, very mystified when I lead them in a certain direction that seems illogical to them. My decision is determined in every instance by the screeching of monkeys, which now seems louder than usual. I feel sure I will find some rewarding mounds.

What does it matter if later Mayan experts accept this statement with a touch of irony? Why shouldn't it be disturbing to think that nobody as yet has established a link between the sites where classical Mayan civilizations developed and the areas where sapodilla trees grow?

What a satisfaction it is to have reached this isolated place where a special kind of vegetation surrounds the dead cities! What a satisfaction, too, to identify the famous coati (*Nasua nasica*), a small, lively sly mammal with the tail of a dog and a pig's pointed snout. These animals travel in packs and climb trees like monkeys. Contemporary ethnographers have noted the presence of the coati in important ceremonies in Yucatán today—on patron saints' days in villages, for example. There is no doubt that it played an important role in ancient Mayan religion.

Julio calls the coati *pisote,* a Nahuati word spread by the Toltecs throughout Central America, where the animal originally was referred to as *chi.* Later, the Spaniards, who had never seen a coati, dubbed it *tejon,* a word which means "shaving brush," and suggests a rather hasty analogy.

This kind of inadequate adaptation of Spanish to Indian terminology occurs frequently in regard to animal names. Confronted by a new, unknown world, the conquerors asked the Indians to supply words for things they had never seen before and then proceeded to interpret such explanations subjectively. Words were often transformed in accordance with the type of ethnocentrism that prevailed during the sixteenth century and that remains widespread even today. Many things in the New World were identified with the aid of Spanish words that appeared to come closest to the meaning.

Actually, but without consciously realizing it, this kind of concrete yet trivial information is what I have come to seek. I long for a living experience on the site; it is not the need for scholarly compilations that urges me on.

But am I not on the verge of adopting a habit common among people who think that they alone can understand because they are lucky enough to be on the spot? Anticipating that I might be defeated in my true purpose here, have I not been seeking false satisfactions to justify my failure? Am I still capable of objectivity?

Little by little, this overwhelming forest is undermining my self-confidence. Our attempts to clear this newly discovered site, which has kept us busy for the last three days, seem to be a struggle against something vague and imponderable. Since our arrival all four of us have been filled with an inexplicable anxiety, although no one will admit it. A curious, oppressive atmosphere hovers over this spot.

A few moments ago we all had the maddening sensation of being under some kind of spell. Twice, in trying to locate the site of a series of mounds near one of our clearings, we lost our way. Twice we returned to our point of departure. Not once before during the last two and a half months had this happened. To make sure that at no time would we lose our bearings, we had always made notches in the trees to mark our passage as we advanced into the forest. We had to feel secure in the knowledge that should it become necessary to find our way out of this labyrinth, we would be able to do so. Now for the first time I have come to share a fear that my companions occasionally experience when faced with certain events seemingly so personalized by fate that they appear to be endowed with a will of their own.

Luckily, Lisandro is shouting; this indicates the direction we should take. He had left us a few hours before to hunt. But the wild game is frightened off by the noise of our activities. Lisandro is calling to say that he came back empty-handed. But he did discover two wells of drinking water. What luck! The river where our camp is pitched dried up after the first heavy rains and is now nothing but a reservoir of mud. We have been forced to dig holes in the river bed to collect enough water for our needs.

Quickly, we hack our way toward the sound of Lisandro's voice. About a thousand feet away are the two wells. The first is actually the mouth of the river, but the second one interests us greatly. It is wider, deeper and, above all, artificial. The

hand of man has been at work here. Buried under the mud I
even discover two stones that seem to have been used as steps!
This is a major discovery because it confirms my suspicion that
the place had at one time been inhabited. Henceforward, it
will cause us to point our search in an entirely different
direction.

The ancient city, whose existence I had surmised, was
probably established on this site because of the presence of
water. Yet for the last three days we unwittingly fixed its
location in relation to our camp. We made our choice by the
merest chance.

We are now blazing a trail to connect the two wells to our
camp. There are three different landmarks to guide us: the
ruins, the camp and the wells.

I spend the rest of the day feverishly figuring out which
direction we should follow in making our clearing. Although
I've drawn up a map, I'm working more or less in the dark
because of my failure to bring sighting instruments along.
Nonetheless, by evening I can say that I have discovered an
important fact. Day after day we have been making a tre-
mendously long detour from our camp to the heap of mounds;
a clearing due east of us will hereafter lead us directly to our
destination.

"Ridiculous! Absolutely ridiculous!" Julio exclaims.

My other two companions agree. When I insist, they go off
into gales of laughter. My theory conflicts with their direct
knowledge of the territory, which is what guided us when we
cleared a path nine hundred yards long. Several times a day
we have traveled that path. The four of us argue heatedly. At
first the trappers speak sensibly enough but soon they become
wild, advancing all kinds of illogical arguments in an effort to
discredit the map I've drawn up. I stand my ground. We must
blaze a trail due east.

For the first time, two different modes of thought meet and
clash. Until now I had adapted myself entirely to the way of
life of these Petén woodsmen. I wanted to learn more about

the forest from them and I was rewarded by a sense of personal enrichment due in part to the friendliness these very likeable men showed me. Their experience enabled me to penetrate deep into this forest, avoiding topographical obstacles, following dried up water courses and skirting the swamps of the underbrush. But barring freak accidents, a compass doesn't lie! Unfortunately, the forest to the east of our camp is far more dense than the area traversed by the path we have been following. This only reinforces the conviction of my companions that a clearing to the east makes no sense.

Tonight, for the first time, there is great tension between us. The unbearable heat foreshadows the rains to come.

This morning, aided by my compass and despite the vehement protests of my companions, we are going ahead full steam in our work of clearing away the hostile barrier of vegetation toward the east. The going is very slow; the difficulties we encounter serve only to confirm the opinion of my chicleros. What we are doing is an affront to their common sense, as if I were forcing the forest to take sides against them. This puts me in a critical position; I feel slightly uneasy.

I had promised the men that if we found nothing today we would return, taking the long way back to the river and the sunlight.

Every blow of the machete brings hope for a miracle, for an unexpected discovery. Already a tunnel about three hundred feet long stretches behind us. Lisandro, in the lead, suddenly halts and the rhythm of his chopping machete also stops. His arm is arrested in midair. Then he quietly puts his machete back into its sheath and slowly shoulders his rifle, which he always takes with him. He fires a single shot. A splendid wild turkey falls into the brambles a few feet away. Having watched the trajectory of the bullet, I rush over to the spot where it fell. You have to act quickly because even a wounded turkey can move very fast. We could lose it in the space of a few seconds. But just as I am about to pick it up, a leopard falls upon it and swiftly vanishes, its prize between its teeth.

All that is left is a pile of rumpled feathers, still warm. Vexed, I return to hear Julio shouting that he has just spotted some honey.

Rey and Lisandro join him. Suddenly a great feeling of lassitude pervades me. Nothing has changed. Food remains the main preoccupation. Does it matter that the men have found honey? All I want to know, and immediately, is whether the clearing will take us to the mounds. If only just once everyone's efforts were focused on that end! Yet my friends are probably right not to lose sight of realities, not to forget even for a moment the need for food. Hadn't I felt that way myself a minute ago, when I rushed toward the wild turkey? Alone and obstinate, I continue working my way due east. In a few minutes the opening I have cleared leads me toward a mound whose vegetation we had cut away only yesterday. Thank heavens for the compass! We had already spent some time examining this very mound, probing and looking. And we had found nothing.

So I sit down on this disappointing hillock, to mark the clearing on the map I have made. Where should I put my compass? There, on this stone? Absent-mindedly, I keep staring at it. Suddenly, I forget everything—notes, maps, plans! I dig feverishly into the surrounding earth. My impatience makes me clumsy. Yes! There it is! A piece of sculptured stone! Marvelous!

I let out a wild, triumphant shout and a great feeling of elation rises up in me.

My stone, my great discovery, seems to be a rather broad step in a staircase. It's about 10 inches high. Sculptured on it is the profiled figure of a man, recumbent, almost naked. His hands are tied at head level to some hieroglyphic writing; he is a prisoner. Is this stair part of a series commemorating a great victory? I shout to my companions.

We all go back to work with enthusiasm. Then I make a second discovery: these rough woodsmen are now digging with great care, as if touched by some sort of grace. Already they have acquired a feeling of awe for Mayan art, although it has barely revealed itself to them.

This is only the beginning. An hour later, as I climb to the top of the highest mound, one stone among a thousand attracts my attention. Scarcely protruding from the spongy earth, it is about two-thirds of the way to the summit of the little artificial mound and about sixty feet from the ground. Ten times at least we have climbed this mound without finding a thing. Why, then, do I glance at this stone rather than at some other? Could I have acquired a new sense, the gift of second sight, during the last few hours? Now I can definitely discern a much clearer structure, even a certain order amid the general confusion of the vegetation.

For a few minutes the forest seems to be a Chinese wishing well, an onyx slab upon which various pictures appear, depending on the identity and psychology of the spectator. Furthermore, when I look closely at the forest, it seems like a kinetic painting in which everything changes according to the position of the viewer. If I look more searchingly, architectural forms appear for a few brief seconds so clearly that I can actually describe them.

We dig away at the periphery of this promising stone. Actually, it is the summit of an enormous monolith, five feet across. At first glance, it seems to be a stone door embedded in casing which at one time must have covered it entirely. We are probably working on the remains of the city's main pyramid which was surmounted by a large temple before it disappeared from view.

We struggle to remove dirt from the door. Little by little it emerges; apparently it was a heavy panel. Soon a magnificent specimen of pre-Columbian art dazzles us: a sumptuous sculpture covering the entire surface of the stone slab and portraying a Mayan priest in profile, intact in all his glory. It is an expression of the purest style, dating from the classic period! In his right hand the priest holds a scepter, symbol of his authority and of his exalted rank in the religious hierarchy.

His left hand is gracefully raised in a gesture of prayer. In many places the bas-relief shows traces of color.

For a long time I stand transfixed before the majesty with which some gifted artist endowed this unknown individual. The priest reigned over the city more than a thousand years ago. . . .

Suddenly I have the feeling that the forest, weary of the struggle, has decided to yield up all its treasures.

VI

Iconography

THE majestic sculptured monolith, which represents my second spectacular discovery, weighs several tons and measures eight feet in height. I am so impressed with it that I find myself imagining it to be the vital clue which will finally enable us to fit together the pieces of the Mayan puzzle.

We finish digging it out from beneath the stone wall that has imprisoned it. The task is so delicate that we have already devoted three full days to it. Actually, the piece is a stela. The tons of material that overhang it seem to press down relentlessly. Now, leaning slightly forward since it has been liberated, it seems to be threatening us. As I contemplate it, I have the feeling that there is something about it which does not tally with my expectations. Viewed in its entirety, it surprises me because of some special quality which I am at a loss to define.

Let us forget for a moment the excitement of discovery, the enthusiasm begotten by the contrast between these exquisite sculptures and their wild setting, for at any second the stela could come crashing against us. We must hurry to anchor it in place.

Julio keeps asking me how a stone weighing so much could

have been raised so high. I assure him that the Mayans knew nothing about crow bars or cranes, that they had absolutely no knowledge of mechanics. So there he is, ready to believe in some magical intervention or divine assistance.

Like most Mayan stelae, the one we have just dug out is made of limestone, usually called soapstone because of its oily, rather soft consistency. It tends to remain soft when buried and to harden when exposed to the air, a phenomenon well known to geologists. In the ancient quarries, the Mayans used large basalt chisels to dig real trenches that served as the periphery of each future stela. Then they would disengage the stone by digging horizontally underneath it. As their work progressed, they slipped round slabs under the block. Once it was loosened, large teams of men especially designated for this task hauled it with ropes made of hemp or liana, while others slipped additional round stones under it to expedite its forward movement.

The sculpturing on the stela was always done after the huge stone had been set in place. The sculptors worked with basalt or diorite chisels—which ranged in size from two to six inches—and with wooden mallets or small cyclindrical stone hammers.

I sit down on a fallen tree and try to view my stela objectively. This, I must admit, is far from easy. I think, however, that I have not so completely taken leave of my senses as to allow my judgment to be warped by over-identification with the object of my discovery.

Mayan handiwork is the only kind of pre-Columbian art that can be easily appreciated by anyone. It remains faithful to the anatomical proportions of man and in this respect resembles the classical art with which we are familiar. It seems to me that this stela, far from representing merely an expression of esthetic feeling, is designed to convey a profound message of sorts whose meaning and purpose escape me for the moment, but which might be a clue to this entire civilization.

Though I am unable to interpret it, this stela is one more

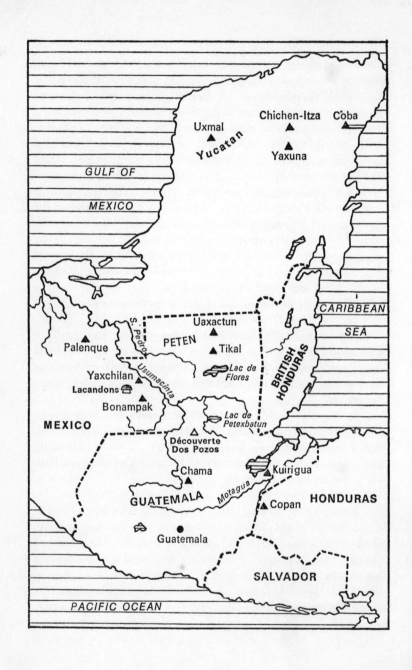

piece of evidence to add to the existing collection of Mayan artifacts identified by archeologists. The latter already has a considerable amount of information. Each new discovery made in the Mayan area, whether an isolated piece or part of a whole series of objects, must be noted and classified.

An extensive study of the various discoveries has enabled archeologists, in theory at least, to divide the Mayan country into five regions:

1. The high plains of Guatemala

2. The valley of Motagua, a frontier region of the south separating Guatemala from Honduras and comprising the ancient cities of Copán and Quirigua

3. Petén, together with Tikal and Uaxactun

4. The valley of Usumacinta, including Palenque, Yaxchilán, Piedras Negras, etc.

5. The entire peninsula of Yucatán, which embraces Chichén-Itzá, Uxmal, Tulum, etc.

Climatically and topographically these five regions are dissimilar. Although certain archeological constants seem to lend them some unity, each region has a distinctive style of its own. The region in which we made our discovery is located far to the south of Petén.

After years of studying the systematic research of specialists and the information available about iconography, I have noted that Mayan artists never illustrate scenes from daily life; in all their works they draw attention to religion and to war. This last point tends to refute the accepted idea that the Mayans were peaceful and opposed to war or violence.

Religious symbols are always associated with a central figure who is never a god but rather a war chief or a high priest performing rites, most of which remain incomprehensible. I can therefore state without reservation that the sculpture of our stela depicts a high priest, hugging to his breast a ceremonial staff, the symbol of his religious position. His features profiled, his arms almost directly opposite the viewer, his feet and legs slightly apart—this person is sculptured in

one of the four typical positions that we find everywhere.
(The three other positions are the face in profile, the arms
directly opposite the viewer, the feet and legs delineated but
never crossed above the knee; the body facing the viewer, the
feet pointed outward and the countenance in profile—this is
the most common position; finally, a position similar to the last
but with the face fully in view.)

In the history of Mayan art, these different positions are not
depicted successively. Consequently, one cannot assume any
definite sequence in the evolution of Mayan sculpture. All of
these positions are to be encountered in any given period.
Certain details in the matter of dress may, however, yield a
chronological clue. The high priest in my stela is wearing
sandals with rough-hewn, jaguar-skin ankle protectors. Such
footgear is also found among certain ethnic groups of the
Chiapos. In any case, this particular detail tells me that the
stone does not date from the beginning of the classical period,
around 300 A.D., but belongs to a somewhat later era.

Only a few meager details of this kind, a few minor changes
in the iconographical composition, indicate development in the
matter of style. The necklaces of important people, for example, did evolve in the course of time. During the early part
of the classical period, these ornaments tended to be narrow
—only four or five strands of beads—little by little they
became more elaborate until finally they covered the entire
chest like breast plates.

Certain areas of the stela still bear traces of red paint. The
Mayans mixed red, which they got from iron oxide, with copal,
a resin they also used for incense. They thus obtained an
excellent colored finish which they rubbed on their monuments. This practice of painting edifices is difficult for us to
imagine; yet it should not surprise us because the Mediterranean peoples have done likewise.

As a precautionary measure, we have decided to build a
prop to prevent the stela from tipping forward. I am somewhat slower than the others in collecting the necessary trees
and branches for this task because ever since yesterday, I have

constantly been taking pictures. Before I could take a few colored slides, we had to cut down a good many of the trees that surrounded the stela. For the first time in perhaps a thousand years, the sun shines on the high priest. But by stepping back only twenty paces, I am in the shadow of the forest. I would like to take some snapshots of this wild vegetation, but the needle of my photo-electric cell refuses to move. There's no light. This is not the first time I have had such an experience: the difficulties of taking pictures in a virgin forest are enough to discourage even the most enterprising professional photographers.

Scarcely had I cut down a few lianas when my companions began to unload heavy branches around the stela. I was just about to join them when suddenly to my left, hardly three feet away, I saw something green and black, a large motionless mass. A snake! Too bad! There was no use wasting film, the light was much too dim. But if it could be transported to the stela where the sun was shining . . . I call out to Rey, asking what kind of a snake it is. Without moving, he answers: "Don't worry, I saw it a little while ago. It's not dangerous."

Reassured, I lunge toward the snake and grasp it below the head with my right hand. With my left, I take hold of its tail. Of course, it wriggles furiously but I hold it firmly away from me. I manage to carry it to our work site. It has a shattering effect on the men. Julio and Lisandro flee as swiftly as their legs will carry them and Rey, his face distorted, shrieks: "Por Dios, no, no! It's not the snake I saw. . . . Be careful! It's dangerous!"

For an instant I remain frozen with fear. Besides, I feel an utter fool. Then, a moment later, I feel like laughing, but there I am, busily hanging on to the accursed snake and trying at the same time to allay the panic I have caused among my companions. What should I do? Mustering all my strength, I toss the reptile as far away as possible and unsheath my machete. Too late! The snake takes off without an instant's hesitation. A narrow escape for both the snake and me!

I do not laugh at the terror of my companions. I know all

too well the kind of fear that snakes, even non-poisonous ones, arouse; for a long time I too was afraid of them. But one day, in the Venezuelan savannah of Guárico, I met an excellent French entomologist who taught me how to handle them. He would catch the most poisonous snakes and the innocuous common garden variety with equal ease. "The main thing," he told me, "is not to be afraid of them. Don't forget that a second's hesitation can mean a serious bite, perhaps even death."

A few months later, on the banks of the Orinoco, I had a chance to verify this. Because I hesitated a few seconds before catching an anaconda, I suffered a deep bite on my right hand.

Apart from the terrible danger snakes actually represent, man seems to have an innate aversion to them. All the mythologies of the world, including those of Scandinavia where few reptiles exist, assign a prominent place to this branch of the animal kingdom. For man the snake has become a demoniacal spirit because of its appearance and its occasionally fatal bite. On the other hand, in certain cultures, it is the symbol of immortality because each year it exchanges its old skin for a newer, handsomer and tougher one. Thus, the ancient Greeks venerated the serpent when they worshipped their ancestors.

The Mayans also venerated it. Their entire civilization centered on the worship of this reptile. It became an obsessive element of their culture. My chicleros are quite surprised when I show them the ceremonial staff held by the high priest sculptured on the stela. It is a representation of a two-headed serpent. The most excitable of my companions, Rey, exclaims that the *antiguos* certainly had strange customs.

I have often studied the multiple expressions of the serpent motif in Mayan art, their varied composition, the transition, whether subtle or abrupt, from a whorl to a straight line in one form of sculpture or another. There is not the slightest doubt that this is a two-headed serpent on our stela. In the jaws of all bicephalous snakes a grotesque human head is always

lodged. I can see the head plainly on the stela although the
design is somewhat lost among the elaborate decorations.
On sculptures of ceremonial staffs the serpent is elongated
and rigid. Why I do not know. In fact everything here is shot
through with mystery. What does the symbol signify? Is it an
emblem of some kind? And why a two-headed serpent?

A thorough examination of the Mayan bas-reliefs shows that
the serpent is the most frequently encountered motif on
masks, sword-belts, headgear and ordinary belts. According to
Tatiana Proskouiakoff, a specialist in the field, the explanation
is the serpent's symbolic function rather than its undulating
form, which constitutes nonetheless an important decorative
element.

Serpent-deities are to be found in all Mesoamerican civilizations. Among the Nahuatls they represent the incarnation of
both water and lightning, sometimes the two simultaneously.
The Aztecs had a whole hierarchy of such gods—serpents
made of obsidian, jade, turquoise and so on—that in many
instances represented deified stars. Frequently the Aztecs surrounded their pyramid-temples with these gigantic stone reptiles. Tenayuca, which the Spanish conquistadors dubbed the
"City of Serpents," is a case in point. And we must not forget
the famous plumed serpent, the incarnation of the god Quet-
zalcoatl.

The frequent appearance of this reptile throughout the
central plains of Mexico, to say nothing of the many meanings
attributed to it, yields no clue whatsoever to the significance of
the Mayan two-headed serpent. A necessary preliminary
would be a clarification of its context on the bas-reliefs. But all
the accessory ornamentation—scepter, sword-belt, sandals,
necklaces—all the symbolic elements, conspire to conceal the
secret. Even the sequence, which might ordinarily be reveal-
ing, remains indecipherable.

My companions have returned. They are still laughing about
the panic caused by the snake. A ray of sunshine bathes the
handsome stone door. We are very proud of ourselves. . . .

"When I think that they fashioned this large piece with

stonecutting tools and wooden mallets!" says Rey, who has great curiosity about everything. "Well, it's just hard to believe!"

I, for my part, am thinking about another major difficulty the Mayan artist must have encountered: that of combining sequence or symbolic meaning with esthetic qualities in order to create a true masterpiece. Often he had to sculpture an object so that it might be viewed from the front and thus be easily identifiable. Its symbolic meaning had to be brought home, even though the logic and perspective of the design would have been better served had the object been presented in profile. The Mayan artists were familiar with foreshortening and balanced proportions, but perhaps they often magnified the size of certain details in order to make them more explicit.

Our stela is an excellent illustration of this difficulty. The high priest's headdress alone takes up two-thirds of the entire sculpture. In fact, this item consists of two superimposed coifs whose back parts are ornamented with the plumes of the quetzal, the sacred bird.

The quetzal is to be found solely in the wooded heights of the Chiapas, in the western section of Honduras, and in Guatemala. It is the size of a parrot, and its tail of two or four feathers may be as much as three feet long. Because of its rarity and beauty, and the splendor of its color, which is green—evocative of the renewal of waters and vegetation—the quetzal's feathers symbolized wealth and abundance. Hence they became an emblem of authority. All the prominent figures of Mesoamerican civilizations were decorated with these plumes. Men have transported them on their backs over thousands of miles. Eventually they came to fetch an exorbitant price. Perhaps the large number of quetzal feathers on Mayan stelae explains the origin of the Plumed Serpent, whose entire body is adorned with the plumage of this rare bird. This famous serpent-deity was first discovered in Teotihuacán, in the heart of the central plain of Mexico, near the present capital. The Nahuatl, Toltec and Aztec invaders adopted it with so much enthusiasm that they ended up by making it their principal divinity. The curious thing, of course, is that all these peoples resided in areas that were separated from Mayan territory by more than a thousand miles. As early as the fifth century, the Teotihuacáns established a very important colony at Kaminaljuyú, on the plains of Guatemala, in order to do business more readily with the inhabitants of the region. It was therefore rather easy for them to obtain the feathers as well as rubber and cocoa from the lower plains. These émigrés had doubtless noticed on Mayan stelae the constant juxtaposition of serpents and quetzal feathers. They apparently proceeded to combine the two symbols and to take them back when they returned to their own areas.

"The bird of the precious plumes," is today Guatemala's coat of arms. The monetary unit of the country also derives its name from it. Although the original Mayan name, "kukul," has been lost, the typically Nahuatl equivalent, "quetzal," has been retained to the present day.

The front and the visors of the high priest's headdress are designed to depict jawless serpents. The eye of the upper animal is adorned with a symbol, %, that is often associated with the god of death, *Ah Puch.*

Like all prominent personages, the high priest wears large earrings, bracelets and a heavy jade necklace. Mayans regarded jade as the most precious of all stones. On the necklace you can see small human heads shaped like those of present-day Jivaros. Were the heads made of jade?

The sword-belt is very important. Wide and decorated with a string of tubular jade stones, it seems quite separate from the person it adorns. In the back, defying all the laws of gravity, a grotesque, highly decorated little human head stands out alongside a slightly saurian beak that might belong to the mythical bird, *moan.* Here, archeology should come to our rescue by giving us some details about the strange belt. Unfortunately, however, no objects of this kind have ever been exhumed from tombs, although they are often seen on pieces of sculpture.

There is no trace of the customary loincloth. The high priest wears a long tunic that appears to be rather stiff, probably because it was padded like a coat of mail.

The sculpture may be rated the work of a great artist because of its profusion of details and its overall effect. The left hand, raised in a sacrificial gesture, is marvelously explicit. This makes me wonder whether the clumsiness of the right hand, with its index finger awkwardly bent toward the thumb, is not meant to convey a special meaning. For some specific reason the artist was obliged to depict the gesture in just this way. It disrupts the harmony of the picture, and the artist knew this; yet he was not deterred. I am convinced that in Mayan art there is an entire language of gestures that the experts have thus far neglected. I first became aware of this when I saw the marvelous multicolored vases of the classical era that came from the summit of Chixoy (Nebaj, Chama, etc.). But in the piece of sculpture we are now considering, what exactly does this lack of proportion signify?

The Mayans had the custom of mutilating their tongues, ears, genitals and fingers in order to extract their blood and offer it to the gods. At Bonampak and at Yaxchilán, on frescoes as well as on pieces of sculpture, the male figures who observe these sacrificial bloodletting rites always wear robes similar to the garment of the high priest of our stela; they are also represented as making gestures similar to his. That's it! Our high priest has just finished offering his blood to a deity. His right index finger, so clumsily presented, is actually broken off. This special kind of mutilation leads me to assume that every self-inflicted wound is connected to a special god or to some characteristic rite, or even to the very function of the person executing the sacrificial ceremony.

Suddenly, having made a minute examination of the figure, one fact seems clear: instead of turning toward the right, like all the figures in Mayan stelae, the high priest gazes toward the left. This explains the strange impression this piece of sculpture made on me when I first looked at it as a whole. Does this deviation from custom mean that the crucial point of the city, its magical center, is to be found toward the left rather than toward the right?

VII

Pyramids and Cities

BURIED in the forest and hidden under the earth, was this Mayan city waiting for us to come upon it and deliver it from oblivion?

I try to picture it during its period of glory, with its temples in vast plazas, its *pelote* ball courts, its astronomical observatory, its esplanades for offerings, for sacrifices. . . . The very existence of this city makes us inventors, since this is the word that designates those who make discoveries, even in archeology and paleontology. The inventors of a Mayan village!

Aware of their new situation, my companions begin to take an interest in everything connected with the history of their ancestors. They want to know everything and believe that I will be able to locate the most important parts of the city. They do not understand the role that intuition, or rather an essentially subjective conviction, has played during these last few days. They also have no inkling of the complexity of Mayan civilization.

Where but in archeology can we obtain some light? Stratigraphy has enabled us to establish an approximate chronology for the techniques employed when the Mayans occupied Petén.

Late in the nineteenth century several cities were discovered. An examination of the findings have clarified problems relating to the origins of this civilization, the reason it was established here and the causes of its disappearance. Yet the cities themselves have remained almost mute on such essential points and questions still remain to be answered. Hence each new archeological discovery gives the man who makes it the heady impression that he perhaps holds the key to all these enigmas.

Things are complicated by the fact that each city is a special case, perhaps the capital of one small state among many others. This diffusion, which may be due to a very special social structure, reminds us of Greek cities of the fifth century B.C.

Moreover, a Mayan city, because of its highly individualistic character, probably did not adopt the architectural canons of its neighbors. It is therefore impossible to compare our discovery with known cities elsewhere. Nor can we make any deductions about the internal organization of a Mayan city since we have no information about its overall schema.

Nevertheless, as I contemplate our marvelous stone door, my imagination runs away with me. I would guess, judging by the sturdiness of the masonry as well as the skill of the sculptor, that under all the humus we will find evidence of an exceptional architectural creation, that temples and monuments of all kinds are laid out functionally and harmoniously in accordance with the design of the builders. But, careful now! Let's not go too far! A Mayan city is not an urban phenomenon. Besides, when the present century began, the word "urbanism" was not included in our dictionaries. This suggests that it is a major preoccupation of our modern world, worried as we are about population growth and housing problems. Did all the cities of ancient Greece and Rome adhere to rigid architectural plans? Even the inexhaustible Vitruvius was not sure. But archeological diggings have revealed that most of them did follow a general plan. When they settled in America, the Spaniards designed their cities on the basis of straight lines, locating their communal buildings, churches and barracks according to a rational plan. Streets, bordered by houses, ran in straight lines from a central square, flanked by wide avenues. A complex urban language was thus created, yet it is one we have no difficulty deciphering.

Nothing of the sort is true of Mayan cities. They do not seem to adhere to any plan or rule. There is no evidence of any attempt to locate the inhabitants as effectively as possible or to plan cities in such a way as to make things easier for their residents. The center of the city, consisting of temples and esplanades, appears to have been uninhabited at all times. Perhaps priests and aristocrats built their clay and wooden structures as close as possible to the religious center, conforming as they did so to the requirements of a well-defined hierarchy. The more important a man's function, the closer he lived to the center of the city. At least, so I presume. But I have no proof that this is so. I base my guess on the history of the Aztecs, who developed such an hierarchical system. If Mayan urbanism conformed to any rules, they still remain to be uncovered.

Another question that still needs to be answered: why have civilian edifices never been erected in the religious cities which the Mayans built in the heart of the forest? Pyramids, temples, arches, roads—these are typical Mayan structures, suggesting a vast technical organization as well as precise knowledge.

It is logical to assume that the architects employed some unit of measurement, some sort of golden rule in building edifices so harmoniously proportioned. This was certainly true of the Egyptians during the ancient era that antedated the dazzling cities erected along the Indus and in Mesopotamia. In Egypt identical wooden moulds were used to shape the clay and straw bricks used in the construction of buildings. As a consequence, the bricks, which were dried in the sun, had an identical form. Very soon they came to serve as models, as a common measure of sorts, a standard unit of length. Quite soon, too, the famous Egyptian triangle appeared. Its measurements—three-four-five—enabled the architects to build well-proportioned edifices.

Nothing of the kind is true of the Mayans. Information culled from our classical education is of no help whatsoever in this Mayan tangle.

Scientific observation does, however, enable us to say that at Uaxactun, the oldest Mayan city known, two temples served as landmarks for the sunset during the winter and summer solstice. At Copán, in Honduras, buildings were constructed with an eye to their observable relation to the movements of the sun. Does this mean that Mayan edifices were constructed solely to serve as landmarks for the sun's movements?

These are questions I have been pondering for a long time. Today I must recapitulate the subject as simply as possible in order to give clear answers to my companions' questions. So here I am, attempting to popularize everything I know about the Mayans. Every detail that impresses me, precisely because of my European education, is to them merely one more fact indistinguishable from all the others. That the arch used by the Mayans in erecting their structures is a unique phenomenon in Mesoamerica leaves them altogether indifferent, whereas I regard it as extraordinarily interesting. The arch is a marvelous example of man's ingenuity in dealing with the problem of gravity. This mass of stone, whose slight beveling enables an entire structure to rise up, which transmits in lateral thrusts the weight it supports, has made it possible to allocate a much greater amount of space to the inner chambers.

Before the Christian era, the Romans, taking their cue first from the Etruscans and then from the Greeks, made full use of the arch. But it was only after they had studied the brick constructions of the Middle East that they conceived the notion of reinforcing the arch with cement—an architectural revolution which resulted in new dimensions for their buildings.

Yet the Mayans also knew how to construct arches with

cement! How did they discover this? Before their advent, no
such arch existed in the Americas. They therefore could not
have borrowed from a neighboring culture. Did they arrive on
the continent already armed with a cultural baggage that
included knowledge of this technique? Is this a rare instance
of imported information that has never been lost?

I find it impossible to communicate my enthusiasm to my
companions. Rey has just remarked laconically: "You can
make anything hold firm if you use cement."

Is this a commonplace? No. His logic forces me to reconsider the question of the Mayan arch.

First, I have to determine its exact nature. Is it identical
with what we usually designate as a cantilever arch? Lacking
in the Mayan arch is the keystone or central voussoir, which
holds the rest in place. Unless cement was used, the arch
could not have held up. The stones making up the side walls
have tenons on the inner facade; this enables them to adhere
better to the mortar in the supports. Bathed in cement, the
Mesoamerican arch, instead of supporting the whole, clings to
it and is encrusted in it. This requires a heavy and cumbersome framework, to say nothing of very hard work; as a
consequence, the angle of deflection is sharply limited. Does
this constitute a flaw? Perhaps. Among the Romans, the use of
cement had the very opposite result. Heavy lateral arches were
no longer necessary and the central arch could be made
larger.

As we have seen, the Mayan arch is not a technical triumph,
although the Mayans were skillful technicians. It is an in-
tegrated part of the entire edifice only because cement was
used. The South American Indians knew a great deal about
mortar, and it is precisely this knowledge that served them
well when they built the Mayan arch.

For the people of ancient Greece and Rome, the arch served
a utilitarian function. This, however, is not true of the Mayan
arch. Was it created in the Americas solely for the symbolic

significance of its form? Is it an archetype—the common model of all humanity so dear to Jung—whose existence, however, cannot be scientifically verified? I am inclined to believe that the similarity we encounter among Mesoamerican and new world forms is something altogether fortuitous, but as yet there is no reliable evidence to support this thesis.

The Mayan pyramids likewise raise all sorts of questions. In Egypt the pyramid was a monumental royal sepulcher, its proportions determined by geometric considerations as well as by sacred numbers. Is this also true of the Mayan pyramid?

The extraordinary discovery made in Palenque by the Mexican archeologist, Ruz Lhuillier, might lead us to say yes. Lhuillier uncovered a secret passageway that led to an arched stairway. It took him three years to clear the passage. The stairway led to a sumptuous funeral chamber whose walls were decorated with stucco bas-reliefs. In the center of the crypt was a stone sarcophagus with sculptures adorning its entire surface. Called the "Pyramid of Inscriptions," it rises to a height of seventy feet above a tomb that reposes six feet below the ground's surface. The layout of the funeral chamber, and the massive stone of the sarcophagus, which could not possibly have been transported through the narrow passageway and staircase, suggest that the pyramid must have been erected as a royal tomb.

Nevertheless, after fifty years of intensive investigation conducted at many different sites, it is clear that Palenque is quite exceptional and that the Mayans used pyramids mainly as complements to their temples. At Uaxactun you can trace the origin of pyramids. There you find a terrace on which the Indians first built a simple wooden temple with a thatched roof. The slight elevation of this strip of land was needed to protect the sacred areas from possible floods. It is also quite logical to assume that the Mayans wanted their temples to rise above their dwellings, a desire we encounter everywhere in the world. At first, the notion of verticality, of height, associated with temples, resulted in a slight elevation of the terraces. Gradually it led to the construction of gigantic pyramids, such as that of Tikal which is 140 feet high.

These elevations are strikingly reminiscent of the ziggurats of the Orient, dating from 4000 B.C. If it were not for the four-thousand-year gap, we might be tempted to accept the diffusionist theories and even those of the Mormons, who claim that the Mayans are descendants of one of the twelve tribes of Israel. Of course, this is pure nonsense.

The Sumerians had to work harder than the men from Petén because they lacked stones and mortar. They had to bake millions of bricks, using bitumen to hold them together, in order to build giant pedestals for their temples.

The Mesoamericans had no such problems. They discovered mortar long before the Christian era, when they initiated their architectural work. The Mayan world literally rests on a limestone bed; the Indians probably discovered lime before they ever thought of building. They began by adding lime to the water in which they cooked their corn, a custom that has persisted throughout Central America and that makes it possible to enrich the food with precious calcium. To obtain lime, the Mayans ground limestone and heaped the grindings onto a huge pile over a wood fire, a practice still followed today by the people of Yucatán. Combustion occurred very slowly. Freed from carbonic gas by the heat, the stones crumbled in the morning humidity to yield that fine white lime which, when mixed with gravel, produces mortar.

The center of the pyramid, its nucleus, consisted of a mixture of stones and highly compressed clay. Held together by cement, the nature of its surface enabled architects to design rather daring structures. The higher the pyramid rose in the air, the greater were the contractions of the center and the thicker the surfaces.

The art of making stairways developed at the same time as this upward thrust; the tread of a staircase soon became inseparable from other structures.

One thing stands out in any study of the evolution of techniques and architectural forms: the Mayans never demolished their old pyramids. Instead, they covered them and built over them, which also explains the continuing vertical thrust of their monuments.

In the beginning, the temple at the top of a pyramid was a simple hut. Progress and time soon transformed it into a stone edifice. The advent of the arch is perhaps due to the Mayans' desire to reproduce in stone the interior of the first temple, itself a reproduction of the family hut with a conical, thatched roof. Crowning the temple was an imposing decorated crest, a very ornate open-work wall whose height often exceeded that of the edifice itself.

The interior chambers have remained narrow and dark. Was this due to the inability of Mayan architects to make better use of the materials at their command? Or was the reason an excessive respect for preexisting forms, endowed as they were with magical significance? Who can say?

The Mayans used a single word, *actun*, to designate both the inside of a temple and a cave. Can this be ascribed to the similarity of luminosity and atmosphere in both places? Or did the inside of a temple really represent a cave, with all the symbolic meaning that this may have possessed?

Will a close analysis of all the known elements of this civilization ever enable us to answer these vexing questions? Or will some accidental discovery provide the key? For the last few months I have been living with the heady conviction that the clues will come from a chance discovery. I am sure that more treasures await me if in my searches I but follow the direction indicated by the gesture of the high priest.

VIII

An Indecipherable Writing

UNDER the tangled vegetation, quite close to the pyramid, are six large blocks of stone lying in precisely the location indicated by the high priest of the stela. Yard by yard we uncover them by digging. I presume that we have now reached the site of the city's great central plaza.

I am concentrating on one of the stone blocks I selected because of the evenness of its elongated shape. Measuring more than seventeen feet in length, it is unfortunately broken in two places. Could this have happened to the stela when it fell?

Julio and Rey offer to help me, and in a few minutes the stone comes into full view. We now begin working with our bare hands. A few vague forms seem to suggest the presence of sculpture. But the motifs that decorated the part of the surface facing the sun have been pitilessly ravaged by centuries of heavy rain.

Employing heavy branches as levers, we turn the heavy monolith over in the hope that the other side, so long protected from bad weather, has preserved some visible traces of bas-relief. A kind of muffled excitement takes hold of me. The physical effort, too . . .

At last! Once again I shout with joy! Yes, a magnificent, profusely ornate figure appears in all his glory. For centuries he has withstood the ravages and rigors of the forest. Once again men are contemplating his incomparable majesty, and somehow it seems as if the figure is alive. He is holding a lance and a shield. This tells us that he was a great war chief. His necklace consists of nine rows of jade beads, another indication of his eminence. Just below these semi-precious jewels, on the clasp of the sword-belt, is a splendid owl, sculptured in full view with wings spread far apart. The owl is very much in evidence, as if it were a major symbol. The owl of Xibalba! I'm amazed. . . . And yet . . .

Xibalba is the lower world, the inferno described in the *Popol-Vuh,* the only Mayan mythical account that has come down to us. The *Popol-Vuh* is a kind of native bible that originated in the plains of Guatemala. It is written in the Quiché Mayan language but in our Latin alphabet, thanks to an Indian aristocrat of the sixteenth century working some fifty years after the Spanish conquest. Inspired by a Mayan codex, it tells the story of twin heroes summoned by the wicked Princes of Death, who reign over the lowlands of Xibalba, to compete in a contest. This sacred ball game is similar to our basketball. A rubber ball was thrown through a stone ring hung vertically on the wall, at a variable height that often exceeded ten feet. The players were forbidden to use their feet or hands. Possessing a major ritualistic importance, the game spread throughout all of Mesoamerica. Every Mayan city had a ball court; here the most powerful magical forces prevailed.

Unfortunately, the twins were defeated in this important game. The people of Xibalba decided to sacrifice them, according to custom; such was the fate visited on the losers. The first twin was decapitated and his head was strung up on a dead tree. Immediately, the branches of the tree grew heavy with calabashes (fat, hard, round green fruits which, when scooped out, are used as gourds). The macabre trophy had made the tree fertile again. The story does not tell us what happened to the second twin.

A few weeks later the daughter of a Xibalba chief, filled with curiosity, decided to do the forbidden and address the tree whose fruit was taboo. Thereupon one calabash answered by asking her to hold out her hand. The young girl readily complied. Then the talking calabash, which was none other than the head of the sacrificed boy, spit on her fingers. This was the final subterfuge to which our hero resorted in order to perpetuate his line.

The father of the young girl soon realized that his daughter was pregnant. Furious, he ordered the Four Owls, the Advisers of the Brave Men, their messengers and sacrificers, to slay the innocent girl. But she managed to conciliate the executioners and escaped the flint knife that was to open her chest and cut out her heart.

The girl fled to the native region of the hero who had impregnated her, but she did not forsake the Owls whose flight to the highlands she was later to facilitate. This passage in the *Popol-Vuh* ends with the story of her two children, both born in the highlands. They, too, came down to Xibalba to compete in a ball game which, thanks to some magical intervention, they were fortunate enough to win. Thus, recounts the *Popol-Vuh*, "the government of Xibalba was defeated as a consequence of the feats of the Begotten Children. The glory of the people of this region was not so great in the early days, but they liked to wage war against other men. Their frightening faces were wicked, it was said that their hearts were full of cunning, that they—both white and black—were envious, domineering. Emulating the Owls, the people of Xibalba rubbed paint over their faces. . . . But their rule came to an end thanks to the Young Master Magician and to the Little Sorcerer."

Can it be that we are at the site of Xibalba, in the city of the Clan of the Owls? My companions are not overjoyed at the thought. On the contrary, they are quite indifferent to the possibility that legend occasionally coincides with truth.

The stone we have pried from the ground is broken at the level of the figure's forehead. In order to contemplate the Owls' war chief, we turn the upper part of the stela over—and note with surprise a series of hieroglyphic writings above the profusely decorated, complicated coif. Long ago, these hieroglyphic writings crowned the site in the central plaza where the stela stood. I can plainly see the numbers—they are distinctly and very skillfully sculptured—that indicate the date the monument was erected.

Feverishly, I launch into a whole series of calculations in my notebook and also in my head. I go over my figures again and again and check them against the stone symbols, in case I have made a mistake. Finally, I proudly announce to my companions that the large stela was sculptured in the eighth century A.D., twelve hundred years ago. At that time this great lord, proud of his coat of arms which depicted the Owl Clan, reigned over the city.

Rey stares at me, stops a moment to reflect, then says calmly: "I really think you're seeing things, or maybe you're tired. The symbols on the stone say 333. Well, what's that got to do with the eighth century?"

Now it's my turn to stare at him, flabbergasted. "Where on earth did you see any such symbols?"

Without a word but sighing as if he were addressing a half-witted child, he points with the tip of his machete to three similar and parallel whorls placed just in front of the figure's mouth. They look like people embracing or—and this is even more curious—several examples of the figure three. So preoccupied was I with the question of the date in hieroglyphic writing that I had scarcely noticed them.

All this arouses little enthusiasm in the other two chicleros. But Rey, who is very outspoken and remarkably intelligent, immediately grasps the meaning of my explanations and readily accepts the fact that the Mayans used symbols very different from our own in counting, as well as a very different system of computation. They employed only two symbols: a dot, which represented one unit, and a bar, which represented five.

"Very clever," Rey declares sententiously. "It's much easier to remember."

As I go on to say that the Mayans invented the cipher, or zero, Rey bursts out laughing, exclaiming: "What's so wonderful about that?"

There is something wonderful about it, Rey. The cipher, or zero, is of major importance; it constitutes one of man's great achievements. You can't have a positional system without the cipher. Neither the Greeks nor the Romans knew about it. A few Sumerian tablets do indeed show the very faint beginnings of calculations based on a positional system. But the calculations themselves were so inadequately carried out that it is very difficult to understand them. Besides, the practice soon disappeared. Generally speaking, the West admits that the cipher originated in India during the fifth century A.D. Was its inventor a mathematician of genius? Or was he merely a learned man who derived his inspiration from a Sumerian tablet that he had miraculously discovered? We simply do not know.

As for history, it teaches us that it was not until the seventh century that the Arabs of Bagdad, translating a Hindu text on astronomy, rediscovered the zero and the positional system that came with it. And not until the seventh century was it introduced in Spain by the Muslims. Thus, it became official in the West thanks to an Arabian arithmetical treatise translated into Latin.

The cipher was not readily adopted. Not until the fifteenth century did it enjoy a general usage throughout almost all of Europe. This shows that on the mathematical level the Mayans were well ahead of all the rest of mankind, for we have proof that they were already using the zero in the third century A.D.

To count, the Mayans used the vigesimal system, but there is no originality in that. All over the world we find evidence of this method of counting, based on the number twenty. Some of the Indian tribes of the Orinoco basin in South America still use it. In fact, it has survived in the Scandinavian languages and even in French, which derives from Celtic. The French say *quatre-vingts, quatre-vingt-dix* (four twenties, four twenties plus ten) rather than *octante* or *nonante* (eighty or ninety) which, quite logically, is used by French-speaking peoples elsewhere—in Switzerland, for example. In Paris there is the famous Quinze-Vingts hospital (fifteen twenties), founded by Saint Louis in 1260 to care for three hundred disabled people. Moreover, many books confirm the fact that during previous centuries people frequently used the term *six-vingt* (six twenties) when they wished to convey the number 120.

It has been said that the decimal system is the one most natural to man because it enables him to count on his fingers. As for the duodecimal system, it probably originated from the twelve lunations of the solar year. But what is the origin of the vigesimal system? The Mayans can answer this question because in their language "twenty" is called *uinal* and "man," *uinic*. What is more natural than to designate man, who is an entity, by the word twenty, given the fact that he possesses four limbs each of whose extremities has five digits?

The Mayans also invented a second way of counting which consists of designating the numbers from one to twenty by a human face that is different for each number. The existence of these two Mayan systems is somewhat reminiscent of the choice we have of writing a number either by spelling it or by using an arabic numeral: one or 1.

We prefer arabic numerals. The Mayans preferred the dot and the bar. Number one they designated by a dot, number four by four dots, five by a bar, and so it went, up to the number nineteen: three bars plus four dots. After nineteen the positional system, made possible by the use of the cipher, intervened.

In our decimal system, arithmetical progression proceeds from left to right. If we add a zero to the right of the number, its value is increased by ten. In the Mayan vigesimal system, mathematical progression proceeds from the bottom to the top. In the lowest position, the dots and the bars have their proper value. But on the first line each number is automatically multiplied by 20; on the second line, by 20 times 20—in other words, 400; on the third line, by 20 times 20 times 20, to make 8,000 ($20 \times 20 \times 20 = 8,000$) and so on.

This system was a thousand times more convenient than other methods used during that same period throughout the entire Mediterranean world. We can't help feeling sorry for the Romans who, through ignorance, were reduced to counting with the aid of an abacus or pebbles. Moreover, the designation of numbers by the use of letters made their system doubly cumbersome. We have only to take a typical example, cited by the mathematician Teeple, a foremost specialist in Mayan astronomy, to make the comparison. To write the number 888 the Romans were obliged to use six different symbols and twelve letters, to wit: DCCCLXXXVIII. The Mayans, on the other hand, used only two symbols and ten letters, to wit:

At our feet, the long stela lies, watching us.

And on the stone are the most mysterious of symbols of this Mayan civilization, the hieroglyphics which, to avoid confusion, the experts call glyphs.

A little while ago I managed to transcribe rather quickly the glyphs indicating the date of the stela—in other words, the calendrical glyphs. All the others along the length of the column are piled up like dead letters. Who among the specialists in the field will ever be able to decipher this hermetic writing for us? How long will we have to wait for the key to these symbols? And finally, who will succeed in telling us the meaning of this mute message so important that men immortalized it by engraving it on stone over a thousand years ago? Eighty years of research! Are we then to despair of paleography?

And yet everything seemed possible in 1880, when Abbé Brasseur de Bourbourg rediscovered *Relación de las Cosas de Yucatán* in the national library of Madrid.

This book was written in the sixteenth century by Father Landa, a Spanish bishop from Mérida, Yucatán. He wanted to show how greatly "the Indians were steeped in error and barbarism." He also wanted to justify the brutal methods that had been used in his diocese to eradicate the Mayan customs and beliefs. In a terrible auto-da-fé, Landa had reduced to ashes all the native books, the precious codices painted with glyphs, all the traditions of a people. Only three relics have survived, and these have been handed down to us by who knows what miracle?

In his work, Father Landa devotes thirty-five pages to a description of Mayan calendars and an abbreviated explanation of how the people of Yucatán wrote at that time. These pages are a major source of information about the classical era of Mayan civilization. The descriptions and drawings correspond exactly with the notational system and the hieroglyphic writings on the stelae of Petén that date from the classical period.

Father Landa's book was long regarded as the "Rosetta Stone" of Mayan writing. This belief was reinforced by a linguistic phenomenon: the fact that the Mayan language had been proof against every attack, every invasion. Although the Nahuatl language replaced the entire Mexican toponymy, nothing of the sort occurred in Mayan territories; yet, as early as the eleventh century, these territories were invaded by Toltec warriors who spoke only Nahuatl. Not only did the Mayans completely absorb the invaders; later, at the time of the Spanish conquest, they even managed to "Mayanize" the Castilian spoken by the Spaniards who inhabited the peninsula. This has no parallel in all of Latin American history. Even today, more than 300,000 of Yucatán's residents still speak Mayan.

The discovery of Landa's book led the experts of the period to assert without hesitation that the hieroglyphic writings in the sixteenth-century calendars and mathematical tabulations were identical with those found on the monuments of Petén, built between the fourth and the tenth centuries. Not only were the two cultures similar, but the languages as well.

The transcription of Mayan calendars and dates has proved to be extremely thorough. In 1887 the German scholar, Ernst Forstermann, clarified every aspect of the classical Mayan system of measuring time and tabulating dates.

Unfortunately, Mayan writing has not fared as well. For this Father Landa is responsible. He was possibly a good bishop according to the standards of his time, but he was certainly no scholar. Instead of trying to understand the internal rules of Indian writing, he thought he was dealing with an undeveloped alphabetical language. He therefore constrained his Mayan informants to explain the phonetic significance of each glyph. Entirely immersed in his own culture, it never occurred to him that he was studying a method of writing very different from his own. This is a fine illustration of what happens when two divergent cultures clash. Landa was trying to force the Indians to give him the key to an alphabet they did not have!

Three hundred years later, this sterile ethnocentrism was destined to lead scholars astray for almost half a century. They had confidence in Landa's assertions because these had proved correct in regard to the Mayan system of computing time. It never occurred to them to seek elsewhere than in the direction the Spanish priest had so fruitlessly followed.

A few decades ago Mayan specialists began to realize their mistake. They found themselves obliged to reconsider the entire problem without further reference to Landa's data. They studied the graphic composition of the glyphs and each of their elements. Trying to determine their sequence, they discovered that some groups of glyphs presumably consisted of sentences. But although these thorough studies scrutinized every detail, they failed to yield positive results. Besides, even if some day the structure and syntax of this writing were uncovered, we would still need to know the method to which they conformed. Are glyphs pictographs, ideograms? Or do they contain the rudiments of a syllabic form of writing? If so, wasn't this form employed to create homophones, that is, words having the same sound but different meanings (*to* and *two*, for example), which, when pictured graphically, could become interchangeable because of phonetic similarity?

Problems such as these have served as a springboard for endless polemics; they have divided researchers into divergent schools of thought. For example, Soviet scholars, who treated every possibility as a potential revelation, sought recourse in cybernetics. They spent two years working at this. Finally, in 1960, they were ready to feed one of the three Mayan codes into a computer. The results proved more than disappointing; they represented total failure. And yet a computer that could come to the aid of historical research would be a wonderful thing. Too bad! I was not, however, entirely surprised by the fiasco.

Like all experts, the Soviets assumed that the Mayan glyphs represented a method of writing consistent with the language, which is identical with the one spoken in Yucatán at the time of the Spanish conquest. This hypothesis was strengthened by two things: the obvious fact that the Mayan language has persisted throughout the centuries and the selection of a codex of Yucatec origin. This last point is significant even though the sacred book had probably been written after the Mayans disappeared from Petén. The glyphs are exactly the same as those on the monuments that date from the classical era. This confirms that the language of the great Mayans was identical with that of the Yucatán Indians, given the fact that the writing was identical. But what this writing seems to represent is a sacred language used only by the elite, the initiated, and known only by them. In its grammatical form and its phonemes, it is very different from the daily idiom used in Yucatán during the sixteenth century and still spoken there today.

The kings and the priests employed the sacred language to conceal their knowledge and preserve their privileges. We have authentic proof of this. In all the manuscripts written in the native tongue immediately after the Spanish conquest, the European alphabet is adapted to the Mayan language; and here we see the magic importance of the verb, which is secret and must be concealed, and which is everywhere stressed. The *Popol-Vuh*, or, "Book of the Quichés," abounds in examples of this kind. The same is true of the books of Chilam-Balam, which are very typical of Yucatán. One of the titles is illustrative: *Books of the Soothsayers about Secret Matters.* The entire work, which runs to seventeen volumes, tells us that all the Indian territories in Yucatán were headed by an *Alachiunic,* or "Veritable Man." At the close of every *katum,* that is, every five years, the Alachiunic's main task was to subject to an official interrogation all the descendants of ancient families who were slated in turn to become leaders of the group. These men were expected to demonstrate the esoteric knowledge which had been secretly handed down from father to son and which was known as the "Language of Zuyua."

In a chapter devoted to this language and to the famous "Interrogation of the Officials," the Chilam-Balam said: "Then they [the ancestors] communicated their secret language." This took place during the initial migrations of the people.

In the course of my long stay among the Mayans of Yucatán, I myself collected the chants of the sorcerer-priests, the *x'*men. These consisted of words in an unknown language whose meaning was totally unfamiliar to the participants. The *x*'men themselves told me that they used the language handed down to them by their forefathers because of its powerful magical effect. They added, however, that they did not understand it.

Can it be that the custom of changing social structures every twenty years explains, at least in part, the obligation felt by the ancient Mayans of Petén to erect new stelae in their cities every twenty years? Or were the new stelae built solely to commemorate an important event?

Or do all the mysterious glyphs and calendrical symbols, which have preoccupied scholars for so long and which demand such exacting erudition, represent the ceremonial "Interrogation of the Officials"? Would it be going too far to regard these enigmatic stelae as representations of Mayan sphinxes that addressed their complicated questions to those who, for the next twenty years, would be called upon to direct the fate of other men?

If we study the books of Chilam-Balam, we see that certain phases of the Interrogations are presented as a series of commandments or recommendations so ambiguous and confusing as to be altogether incomprehensible. Take, for example, the Interrogation of the Officials cited in the Chilam-Balam of Chumayel. The following is the sixth and clearest question: "Let them go and search for a tree branch covered with pochote thorns, and three twisted things and a living liana to make me a succulent meal for tomorrow. I want to eat it. Who knows if it is harmful to eat the trunk of the pochote?" That was the question. The answer goes something like this: "Here is the trunk of the pochote, the lizard. The three twisted things are the tail of an iguana; the living liana? The intestines of the pig; the bark of a pochote tree? The trunk and tail of a lizard . . ."

These hermetic sentences were spoken and perhaps written in a sacred esoteric language such as Zuyua. If this is correct, how then are the glyphs to be transcribed?

Fortunately, we are not left completely in the dark. Half of the glyphs have already yielded up their secrets. But these have to do with symbols on the calendars. It is significant, however, that inscriptions on the stelae always consist of a series of dates. This is a clue worth thinking about.

In this isolated forest ideas occur to me that I had never entertained before. Can it be that the solution to the mysterious problem of the abandoned villages of Petén is concealed in the consecutive calendars and in the methods of computing time—both salient features of this enigmatic culture?

Can it be that I am halfway toward a definitive understanding of the Mayans? Decidedly, I must ponder more carefully this fascinating subject of time; it strikes me as being the motive power of this civilization.

IX

Mayan Calendars and Time

THREE stelae are lying on the central plaza. We have no difficulty uncovering them. Our discovery has a certain logic about it: the Mayans were obliged to erect a stela every twenty years.

After removing the earth from the stelae and examining them thoroughly, I note with surprise that in falling, all of them moved in the same direction. It does not seem as if they toppled over gradually, over a period of centuries; nor do they appear to have fallen because of some accident. It seems more likely that they were deliberately knocked over, struck from behind. Lying there face down, have these symbols of time lost all significance?

Time. It was the principal preoccupation of the Mayans, almost an obsession. No other people in the world, I believe, has ever been as dependent on time as these Indians of the Petén forest. It was the touchstone of their culture. They created their own mathematical and writing methods in order to measure time, to mark it off. The accuracy of their astronomical observations sprang from this passion. They had to know the time of the sun, of the moon, of Venus, to say

nothing of the all-important Sacred Almanac time. By recording on stone the passage of this inexplicable element, as
imperceptible as life itself, the Mayans felt sure they could
make time coherent and understandable. Furthermore, by
marking it on calendars, they could apprehend the present,
transcend it and thus avoid anxiety. They believed that calamities were sent by time or by gods dependent on time; to
know about the future was also to anticipate it, to attentuate
its effects or escape from them with the aid of religious rituals.

Anxiety and attempts to overcome it are as old as man. At
the very dawn of civilization the Chaldeans developed a
scientific astronomy of their own with the object of perfecting
astrology, that amazing technique for anticipating the future.
Many astrologers and clairvoyants today still use the signs of
the zodiac invented by the Chaldeans thousands of years ago.
Later, it was taken up by the Greeks. Nonetheless, it would be
risky to try to establish a link between the astronomical science
of the Mayans and the astrological science of the Mesopota-
mians. Both peoples observed the passage of time and the
progression of the stars with great precision, but their methods
and calendars differed markedly.

The Mayans invented a solar "civil" year of 365 days. We
know, however, that they made calendrical emendations and
developed a more precise notion of solar time than that
embodied in our own calendar. Thus, the true sidereal year
(that is, the exact amount of time it takes the earth to revolve
around the sun, as determined by the precision instruments of
modern astronomy) consists of 365.2422 days. In our Gregor-
ian calendar—making due allowance for leap years—the year
has 365.2425 days, while the year of the ancient Mayans
numbered 365.2420 days.

The accuracy of the Mayan calculations is all the more
extraordinary in view of the fact that they had no knowledge
of glass and therefore had no precision instruments at their
disposal. (Were the lengthy tubes of jadeite uncovered in
excavations used as telescopes?) In addition, the Mayans had

no clocks, no hourglass, no clepsydra (water clock) with which to count hours and minutes—nothing that could help them to collect exact astronomical data. Well, then?

After deciphering in the only three codices still extant all the symbols connected with the computation of time, we learn that the Mayans never ceased throughout the centuries to study astronomy. Their observations were recorded carefully and exactly on long strips of flattened bark rubbed with limestone and folded like an accordion. These are called codices.

Such persistent observation enabled the Mayans to go so far as to predict solar eclipses.

Their solar year, or Calendar Round, of 365 days, consisted of 18 months of 20 days each and one additional month of 5 days. Each month had its own special name, and each day was numbered from zero to nineteen. The last month, *Uayeb*, was numbered from zero to four. In this calendar the Mayans counted the days as we do the hours, starting from zero rather than from one.

This Calendar Round was inseparable from the Sacred Round, or Sacred Almanac, which the Indians called *tzolkin*, and which consisted of 260 days but was not based on any astronomical observation; in both, time elapsed in parallel fashion, simultaneously and continuously.

When I first learned about this method of computing time, it seemed extremely forbidding. With little conviction, I accumulated books that deal with the problem. Was it really necessary, I asked myself, to study this calendar thoroughly in order to achieve a better understanding of the Mayans? Today, in the presence of these numerous calendrical glyphs on the stelae I have just uncovered, the answer is obvious. Knowledge about the reading of the calendars is the royal road, the only one that will lead straight to the heart of the classical Mayan world. The mania of the Indians for synchronizing their calendars, for uniting them in the alchemical sense of the word, in order to determine all their points of coincidence and to fix their meeting in time—this is something that has not been sufficiently emphasized, as we shall see later.

The fusion of the Sacred Round with the Calendar Round takes place this way: Both begin at the same starting point. Then, 18,980 days elapse before the first 2 days of these calendars again coincide—in other words, there is a lapse of time amounting to seventy-three Sacred Round years, or fifty-two solar years. All this seems so remote from our own conception of time that it is quite difficult at first to understand the Mayan mechanism.

We might try to explain it in terms of the old bicycles that our grandfathers rode so proudly at the start of this century. The large front wheel would be the Calendar Round, divided by spokes into 365 equal parts, each representing a day. The smaller rear wheel, with its 260 spokes would represent the Sacred Round. On each of the two wheels one vertical spoke painted red would mark the day when both calendars began. The cyclist, riding very slowly, would then note that the two red spokes would be back at their respective starting points (of course, after both wheels had traveled an equal distance) when the big wheel had turned fifty-two times and the little wheel seventy-three times.

Here we have, reduced to simple terms, the basic principle governing the synchronization of the two different Mayan calendars. We can be sure that for the Mayans the process had a deep significance. If we pay close attention to it, the endless combinations involved are quite enough to make us giddy.

Speaking practically, each day of the fifty-two-year cycle (seventy-three Sacred Round years or 18,980 days)—the ideal life span of man, according to the Mayans—possessed a magical quality entirely measurable and exact, thanks to this system. We do not, however, know the word for this important cycle of years.

For additional information, one is tempted to go to Aztec historical sources dealing with the same subject. Such a procedure would, in this instance, be quite justifiable, considering the fact that the Aztecs got their calendars from the other peoples of central Mexico who in turn had borrowed theirs from the Mayans, the originators. To be sure, a symbol or rite is often modified when it is transmitted from one ethnic group to another; but it is simply not possible to alter anything as mechanical and precise as a calendrical system.

Unfortunately, a study of the Aztecs sheds very little light on this point. The fact of the matter is that the Aztecs had in effect limited their cosmic vision to the single fifty-two-year cycle. In their thinking, the termination of this major period heralded the possible end of the world. At fifty-two-year intervals a kind of generalized anxiety would take hold of the entire community. People would hide in their huts; priests would walk in procession to the hilltops in order to interrogate the heavens. Offerings and sacrifices were made in the hope that all the planets and stars would continue on their appointed rounds, and that the gods would allow men to live through yet another fifty-two-year cycle on earth. Fortunately, the world did not come to an end. In exchange for this reprieve, the Aztecs were expected to break all their pottery and to burn their old clothes. Not a single kitchen utensil was to be saved from the general destruction. With all due ceremony, a fresh fire was built by rubbing a small stick against a branch of the cocoa tree. Then the people gathered to erect a new temple on top of the pyramids built by their ancestors. Tradition demanded that they refrain from demolishing any former place of worship. This proved a boon to archeologists in their efforts to establish a chronology for the civilization of the Aztecs. At Tenayuca, for example, five structures were discovered, one superimposed on the other, and all of them built above the very large original pyramid.

The Mayans surpassed our limited view of time, fixing the year 3113 B.C. as their point of departure. They thus devised a definite chronology for historical time long before the West. It

was not until the fifth century A.D. that the Christian world—
influenced by a Scythian monk—decided to calculate time
from the date of Christ's birth. The Greeks, for their part,
computed time by olympiads, that is, by four-year cycles, and
the Egyptians dated their history from the beginning of each
dynasty.

The starting date of Mayan chronology, so distant in time,
was obviously chosen because of some historical event; there is
a vacuum, a complete and utter silence for the more than three
thousand years that separate 3113 B.C. and the first date
inscribed in stone. The earliest archeological relics date from
500 B.C. Judging from the results of excavations, it is not at all
likely that the Petén Indians of that era knew how the Mayans
were later to compute time. Specialists in the field are inclined
to think that the year 3113 B.C. signalized a mythical rather
than an actual occurrence. My own private opinion is quite
different, and I will return to it later. For the time being it is
important to realize that if the Mayans had limited their
computation of time to the fifty-two-year cycle, it would have
required seventy glyphs to record a single date, beginning
from their chronological starting point! How complicated it all
is!

At this point the ingenious vigesimal positional system
makes its appearance. To begin with, the Mayans gave each
line of their vertical figures a characteristic name, illustrated
by a glyph, thus avoiding the obligatory upward thrust. But to
harmonize their computations with the calendrical realities of
the 365-day solar year—at least this is an assumption com-
monly made—they changed their figures slightly. For
example: on the second line, the multiple called *tun*, instead of
having its designated value of 20 times 20 equals 400, became
20 times 18 equals 360. The result is:

- $= 1 \times 20 \times 18 \times 20 \times 20 = 144{,}000$ days or one *baktun*
(fourth line).

- $\bullet$ $= 1 \times 20 \times 18 \times 20 = 7{,}200$ days or one *katun* (third line).
- $\bullet$ $= 1 \times 20 \times 18 = 360$ days or one *tun* (second line).
- $\bullet$ $= 1 \times 20 = 20$ days or one *uinal* (first line).
- $\bullet$ $= 1$ day or one *kin* (bottom line).

The priest-astronomers followed these rules. At the end of each katun—approximately every twenty years—they had sculptors engrave on the appropriate stelae indications of the amount of time that had elapsed between 3113 B.C. and the current date. This interval, computed in accordance with the rules for the 365-day solar calendar—or Calendar Round—and synchronized too with the Sacred Round Calendar, was indicated by seven glyphs, in conformity with the vigesimal system. The sixth glyph indicated the Sacred Round; the seventh indicated the day of the month on which the new stela was erected.

Employing this procedure, we would write the date of July 14, 1969, for example, as follows: 1 thousand + 9 hundreds + 6 tens + 9 units of years from our starting point to the fourteenth day of the month July, a day the French commemorate.

The method was called the "Long Count" or "Long Round," and the seven glyphs needed to indicate the date were called the "Initial Series."

In the light of all this, the twentieth-century experts figured out the dates engraved on the stelae. They noted the existence of certain rules governing the general arrangement of the calendrical glyphs and this greatly facilitated their task. Thus, for example, the five multiplier glyphs needed to calculate a certain number of days beyond the chronological starting point generally topped two columns that were to the left of the symbols. Scholars soon came to realize that it was much easier to read the figures if they began at the top and read from left to right. It was no longer possible to make mistakes because the multipliers were no longer expressed by the elevation of their position but by glyphs. The sixth glyph, indicating the Sacred Round, was usually placed in the sixth position; the seventh, indicating the day of the solar calendar, was at the very bottom of the right column.

When I examined the first stela which we had discovered in the central plaza of the city, I very soon noticed that the calendrical glyphs were arranged according to the established pattern. What luck! It was therefore not difficult to figure out the date on which the stela had been erected.

In the upper left-hand corner of the stone, a glyph without a number was engraved. Because of its shape and position, it is called the "introductory" glyph. Preceding all Mayan dates, it scarcely varies in form. The only change is at its center where the image of the god changes because each month is represented by a special god, and it took many months to build the stela. The introductory glyph signals the beginning of the Initial Series. To its right, above the second column of symbols, there are four dots and one bar, in other words, the number nine, coupled with baktun, the multiplier glyph.

On the left-hand column, under the introductory glyph, are three bars, representing the number fifteen, together with the glyph katun. To the right of it are four dots, or four added to the glyph tun. Below them, in the left-hand column, is one dot, or a one in the middle of two zeros (perforated dots) and one bar: five coupled with one and the multiplier uinal.

On the right-hand column: four dots, or a four coupled with kin.

The following, then, is a transcription of the date:

$$
\begin{array}{lrll}
9\ \text{baktun} & 9 \times 144{,}000 = & 1{,}296{,}000\ \text{days} \\
15\ \text{katun} & 15 \times 7{,}200 = & 108{,}000\ \text{days} \\
4\ \text{tun} & 4 \times 360 = & 1{,}440\ \text{days} \\
6\ \text{uinal} & 6 \times 20 = & 120\ \text{days} \\
4\ \text{kin} & 4 \times 1 = & 4\ \text{days} \\
\hline
& & 1{,}405{,}564 & \text{total days}
\end{array}
$$

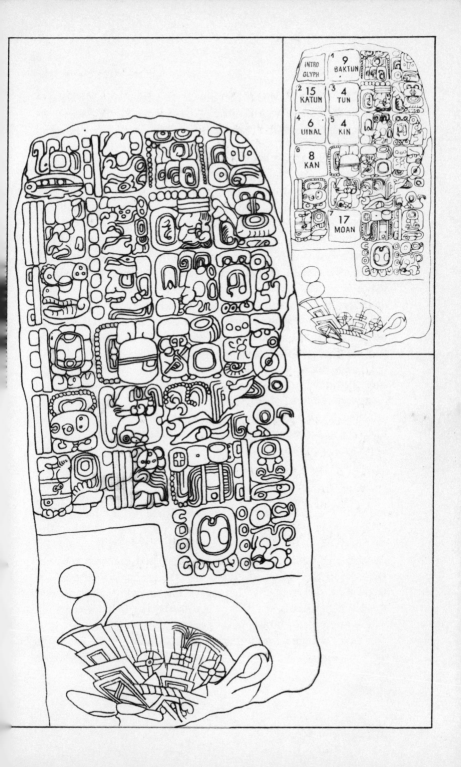

I still had to divide this number of days by 365 to obtain the number of solar years that had elapsed from the beginning of Mayan chronological time until the date on which the stela was erected.

1,405,564 divided by 365 equals 3,850 years and 314 days.

What does this signify in relation to our own chronology? The Mayans' point of departure was 3113 B.C. If I deduct 3,113 from 3,850 years plus 314 days I get 737 years and 314 days. In other words, the stela was erected in 738 A.D.

In my rapid summary calculations, I neglected to count the leap years, which results in a margin of error of a few years. I was familiar with the famous works of Teeple that demonstrate the existence of a "Supplementary Series" in several hieroglyphic writings. These additional days prove that the Mayans knew how to compute true solar time precisely. But the quest for such a Supplementary Series is a laborious job that should be undertaken only by specialists.

One of them, J. E. Thompson, sought to fix with exactitude the date sculptured on our fine stela. According to the Goodman-Thompson correlation, it is 736 A. D.

Actually, there are two types of correlations. They spring from two different theories about precisely when Mayan chronology begins. One of these correlations, that of Thompson and Goodman (3113 B.C.), is generally accepted today. The other is that of the American, Spinden. He sets the starting date back 260 years to 3374 B.C. These 260 years constitute a "katun wheel," a calendrical cycle that I shall discuss later. The Mayans of Yucatán were using it when the Spaniards arrived. No matter which of these two theories you accept, the total number of years that had elapsed between the date of the inscribed glyphs and the chronological point of departure still remains the same. The starting point would simply have occurred either 260 years earlier or later than the beginning of our chronological point of departure.

I have, of course, no intention of mentioning these problems to my chiclero companions. I know how very boring these details can be for the uninitiated. But in the face of this proof, inscribed in stone, of the genius of the Mayans, how can I resist?

Gradually my joy is somewhat tinged with regret. As yet there is no answer in my discoveries to the various questions about the men of Petén that I have been putting to myself.

While grappling with the dates of the glyphs on the stela, I had paid virtually no attention to the last two symbols. It is only now that I notice them. There they are, in the place assigned to them by tradition: the sixth position, the day of the Sacred Round calendar, 8 *kan;* and there, at the bottom of the right column, the date of the Calendar Round: 17 *Moan.*

If I count in reverse the Sacred Round days inscribed on all the dates of the classical period—in other words, if I follow the Sacred Round time inscribed in the sixth position on the stelae, I always arrive at 4 *Ahau;* if I do the same thing with the seventh glyph of the series, the day of the month, I always stop at 8 *Cumku.* Why 4 Ahau and 8 Cumku? This is a mystery.

As for the chronological point of departure, the Mayans always fix it at the end of baktun 13. Why baktun 13? Nobody so far has been able to explain this. It is a Mayan idiosyncrasy always to compute time from the end of a period. Here again questions arise and the quest for answers should prove interesting.

X

An Unfinished Staircase

A WEEK of persistent searching encourages us to map out a highly promising work plan. Our discoveries are proceeding more rapidly. I now have a much more precise notion of the city which, bit by bit, we are extracting from the forest.

On three separate occasions we uncovered stone stairways with four sculptured steps each, apparently an architectural peculiarity of these parts.

Such unremitting labor makes life harder for all of us. Julio, the enthusiastic hunter, keeps forgetting to hunt even though we are badly in need of food. He scarcely takes more than an hour off each day to kill one or two monkeys. These animals now constitute our basic menu. But tacitly we avoid the subject because we're a little ashamed. Monkeys are the kind of game trappers usually scorn; in fact, they are taboo. The flesh of the spider monkey, plentiful in this part of the forest, has a sweetish and loathsome taste. But we have long since ceased to be bothered by such things.

At my suggestion, Julio has stopped shooting female monkeys which, at this time of year, carry their babies on their backs. A few years ago a real slaughter took place here. Hunters shot female monkeys in order to pick up their babies alive and send them to American laboratories where they fetched a good price. Unfortunately, half of the wretched little beasts, unable to recover from the shock of the sudden fall, perished.

The day before yesterday, however, Julio returned to camp with an adorable but terrified black baby spider monkey. Grinning, he handed it to me. His gesture touched and surprised me. Had Julio killed a female monkey?

"Here," he said, "soon our trip will be over. Take this along as a souvenir of Petexbatun."

Suspecting a joke, I replied, "Aren't you doing this because you'd like to see a Frenchman struggle through the forest with a monkey on his back?"

Nothing is more cumbersome and difficult than to walk in the forest carrying an animal like this one. It clings to your hair and hangs on to the branches above the footpath. It also causes a sudden weight to fall on your bag, thus making you lose your balance. I had very vivid recollections of similar misadventures and was not in the least eager to repeat them.

Julio, however, promised to take charge of the little monkey until we got to the river, and so I readily accepted his gift. As if understanding that it belonged to me, the poor beast took refuge in my arms, moaning. After that it refused to leave my side and shrieked loudly whenever one of the others approached. What a mess when I lay in my hammock that night, after carefully packing the little monkey into a pocket of my bag! The animal seemed perfectly comfortable there, but it had refused to eat anything we offered it. That night it began to emit such terrible cries that I finally gave in and, to the amusement of my companions, took it into my hammock. Oh, what a terrible night! By two in the morning the situation had become unbearable. I woke up my three friends to consult them. Should we turn the little monkey loose in the forest?

This would mean certain death because of the wild animals around. Could it find food on its own, without its mother? I doubted this very much.

The four of us suddenly decided to tether the little monkey near our camp in order to save it from possible attack by roving ocelots or hungry jaguars. I tied it up very loosely so that it would not strangle itself in struggling to break free. Thereupon Rey did something that surprised me. From his bag he took a big red handkerchief. Cutting off a piece of it, he tied it around the neck of the little spider monkey.

"That's the custom," he told me. "If you want to protect a wild animal that you're planning to tame, you have to tie a piece of red material around its neck. This will keep danger and evil spirits away."

By dawn the little monkey had disappeared. Absorbed in our archeological investigations, we soon stopped talking about it. . . .

We are still making discoveries, less spectacular ones than before, to be sure, but nonetheless interesting. At the foot of the large pyramid that faces the central plaza, we have just unearthed a small stela.

As I scrape the pedestal, the tip of my machete suddenly knocks against a rather surprising piece of jade, about the size of four fingers. Uneven in form, it is nevertheless sculptured. This modest windfall delights me. One surface exhibits a seated figure, legs crossed, represented in profile. The engraving is superficial, hardly penetrating the stone. But what pliancy in the lines that undulate, straighten out and curve again! Across the entire length of the other surface runs a beveled groove. Seemingly, the artist had given up the idea of engraving the piece of jade and had decided instead to cut it into two parts and use it for something else. I keep looking at this crack and can imagine the effort it must have cost the artist to work on the stone. Actually jade is so hard that it resists even the sharpest of diorite chisels. The artist had only half begun his attempt to split the stone. Using an ancient rubbing technique, he dipped very taut string in wax and fine sand. He should have used the same technique on the other surface of the stone if he intended to break the jade in two. How many days of incessant labor would it take to break a little slab like this? Was the artist discouraged by the prospect of having to rub the stone endlessly? I don't think so. Rather, a certain fear may have stopped him just when he was about to begin work on the design of a god. The jade itself, on which he must have worked daily, was delicate, even hazardous to handle. Even the greatest chiefs venerated this particular variety of stone.

Unlike Chinese jade, which is a form of calcium, American jade consists of sodium aluminum silicate. Actually, it is jadeite. Rarely encountered on the continent, it can be found in the form of boulders in beds along the banks of rivers. The stone is very difficult to spot. Mayan society probably had guilds of specialists who hunted and worked on jade and enjoyed a highly prized magico-religious status.

To complete a single jade sculpture required years of work. The very nature of the round or tubular jade beads in the necklaces of the chiefs testifies to the painstaking work lavished on them. The holes through which the necklaces were strung were probably made with a wooden drill dipped in sand or powdered obsidian. As the artisans worked they stuffed the holes to shape them, then removed the stuffing and widened them gradually. The bead would be drilled piecemeal, first one half, then the other, until the entire bead was perforated. Each hole had the form of an hourglass. The shape is so characteristic that it enables us today to distinguish genuine ancient jewelry from imitation, both of which are sold for an identical sum by people who steal from the tombs.

Lisandro rushes over to me. He has just discovered a number of flagstones, arranged in orderly fashion and only thinly covered with humus.

"It's like a walk," he says, "and I have the feeling that it leads to the small hill over there, behind the large pyramid."

I'm not particularly surprised by Lisandro's find. It does indeed appear to be a flagstone walk rather than a road, which it might well have been. The Mayans, who had no draft animals, often built roads (*saxcab*). Constructed with cement and laid out in a straight line, these roads sometimes rose as much as nine feet above the ground. Due mainly to the fact that they were more than fifteen feet wide, they had a certain elegance. Some, like the one at Cobán, were as much as sixty miles long and connected cities with one another. But Mayan specialists claim that the roads actually served no useful function. Large numbers of people used them only when important religious processions took place.

The roads were paved with flagstones over which limestone gravel was strewn and then pulverized with huge, extremely heavy stone rollers. Close to the Mayan road outside the holy city of Coba and not far from the borders of Quintana Roo, archeologists found one of these stone rollers. It was twelve feet long, twenty-five inches in diameter and weighed five tons. The strength of at least fifteen men was needed to pull it. Did the inhabitants of our city use a roller of this type to prepare the sacred walk that led from one temple to another? Only extensive archeological research can provide an answer to this question.

Thus, contrary to established notions, the Mayans knew how to build roads. This knowledge they shared with other Central American peoples. In the Museum of Jalapa in Veracruz, I admired and photographed an extraordinary little pre-Columbian terra cotta whistle. Shaped by the artisan to look like a dog, it was mounted on four wheels. Here we have definite proof that the wheel was known to the Indians of Mesoamerica prior to the arrival of the Spaniards. The works of the American archeologist, G. E. Ekholm, also bear this out.

The little whistle at Jalapa was a simple traditional object. As for the Mayan road roller, it was not a genuine wheel but a rolled cylinder somewhat similar to the smaller round bars the Mayan Indians slipped under stelae to move them. The question naturally arises: why did the Mayans never use the wheel? Lack of technical imagination? The absence of draft animals? But men could have been substituted for animals, as they were at Cobán. Is it possible that the Mayans were deterred by the fact that the wheel symbolized the sun's image?

The flagstone walk of our city begins at the foot of the monticule where Lisandro dug out an upright stela he had spotted in the morning. It rises in front of the pyramid, still topped with branches, twigs and lianas.

Strangely enough, Lisandro's stela is bare, entirely smooth on all sides. There is no sign of any writing. Was it once covered with stucco, that very delicate plaster mixed with resin which the Mayan sculptors liked to work with? Magnificent stucco bas-reliefs on the facades of temples were discovered at Palenque. But here, where we are, they must have crumbled.

Lisandro and I are trudging the flagstone walk which is quite easy to see under the mud. After about 160 feet, it brings us to the foot of a mound. Approximately eight feet high, the mound occupies an area of about forty square yards. It is late afternoon. Perhaps we are tired. Our imaginations are not fired by the sight of the mound. Yet if processions of priests decorated with colored plumes used to move down this path to the accompaniment of the muffled sound of wooden trumpets punctuated every now and then by the rumble of deer-skin drums, this mute pedestal must surely have been important.

Well, let's get on with our investigation! I call to Rey and Julio. If the four of us work together, perhaps our spirits will revive. Julio is the first to call our attention to a large stone lying at our feet. Rectangular in form, it is smooth and devoid of sculptured figures. Was it brought here by someone who planned to construct a building of some sort? Carefully, we dig up the earth around it with our machetes. We find another, similar stone, and yet another. After two hours of solid digging, we have uncovered a stairway. It has four wide, plain, well-placed flights, three of which are ornamented with sculptured bas-reliefs. I look at the stairway carefully. It seems unfinished. A stone is missing from the fourth step. Oh, there it is. It's the slab Julio found at the outset. Also devoid of sculptured figures, it is ready to be set in place; in fact, it has been waiting for centuries. The sculptures on the third flight appear to be incomplete. We can visualize the glyphs to the left of us, although they have been scarcely begun. Far to the right we can see the place prepared for the installation of the slab. There is no doubt at all that this stone staircase was abandoned in the midst of its construction. We have the feeling that the workers, the artists, were seized with a sudden panic and fled as quickly as they could, leaving their tools behind.

Scenes of court life in bas-relief appear on the central stones of the completed flight. I note with surprise that the heads of all the figures have been badly mutilated and that their features have been chipped or broken with some heavy object. It must have taken a ferocious rage to destroy faces like these, destined for posterity. The condition of the flights of stairs, our latest discovery, greatly disappoints my companions. But I am very excited. What a marvelous find! For the first time in the history of Mayan archeology we have uncovered clear evidence that a classical city was once abruptly abandoned. This is the final gift to us from the forest of Petexbatun!

Our bags are closed. A branch, the last, is slowly burning on the hearth of our camp. Our great adventure is drawing to a close, but we are not sorry. The ticks and mosquitoes have become increasingly ferocious during these last few weeks. Every day an unrelenting rain has made the earth so soft and spongy that it is impossible to squat on the ground for our meals. Our clothes and our hammocks—everything, in fact—is beginning to mildew. We feel as if we are disintegrating. Water seeps in and remains; it is everywhere.

For the past three days, Julio has had to resort to an old chiclero trick in order to light our fire. He pulls from his pocket a piece of rubber he had taken from a rubber plant a long time back. I had wondered about it at the time. He cuts off a small piece and applies a match to it under a pile of brushwood and damp branches. Thanks to this piece of slow-burning rubber, the wood finally catches fire.

Lisandro, his machete in hand, takes the lead. I'm in my old position, walking second in our single file. I feel as if I'm immersed in a steam bath. I can hear Julio's steps behind me. Drops of sweat are running down my forehead, already obscuring my vision. But I do not take my eyes from Lisandro's heels as he quickens his pace.

And now the long monologue I carry on with myself resumes and accompanies me during these interminable, difficult walks. I think about all the marvelous discoveries we have just made. We are the victors of Petexbatun! I smile complacently to myself for a minute. Suddenly I remember the documentary slides I had taken. Will they come out? Was my film damaged? What incidents await us on our way back, or on the river? The return will be just as difficult, just as full of pitfalls, as our trip out.

Once again I think about the Mayan city which in the end I baptized Dos Pozos because of the importance of the two wells. Since Mayan pyramids are not tombs, can it be that the extraordinary door of the sepulcher is in reality a monumental panel? And what about the stelae in the central plaza? How enthusiastically they will be received by people who care about Mayan art! As for our latest discovery, the unfinished stairway, doesn't it perhaps possess a special significance? It is unique insofar as it provides tangible evidence of the death of a classical city, a demise caused by some terrible shock. Upon reflection, I think I have the explanation for that stone door, or panel, almost entirely covered with masonry. Very probably it was part of an earlier structure. The architects were busily covering over the entire edifice, as required by custom at certain specified dates. Their object was to construct a larger pyramid and to build a new, more sumptuous temple on top of it. And then something terrible happened to interrupt the work. It was this, perhaps, that enabled me to uncover the upper end of the monolith. But what calamitous event could have occurred to precipitate so sudden a departure from the city? Announcement of the advent of a new dynasty that might have been particularly unpopular? The furious blows that obliterated the faces of the sculptured figures on the steps of the stairway seem to point to an uprising rather than an invasion.

But how could so much turmoil arise in a very disciplined, organized society, one that had attained such a high level of civilization? This time, at least, I am bringing back to the world not only a new city but unusual information that will prove sufficiently reliable, I trust, to warrant the attention of specialists in the field. Once again they will be able to look into the question of how the great Mayans disappeared. Will I myself find the key that can resolve this mystery?

The monkeys are shrieking furiously and the noise they make suddenly interrupts my reverie. We have just disturbed a couple of black spider monkeys. I stop Lisandro, who is about to take aim. No, no more of that. We have enough grilled meat to take care of all our needs until we reach the river. Once there, we will have plenty of fish to eat. A small dark mass approaches the scandalized pair shrieking up there in the trees. I must be dreaming! It's a little spider monkey with a red ribbon around its neck! Here is my souvenir of Petexbatun, in perfect health! It had found parents to adopt it. After every leap from branch to branch, the two adult spider monkeys turn around to see if the little orphan is following them. Whenever necessary, they patiently wait for it. A ripple of emotion runs through our group. Well, that's fine! I don't need a monkey as a souvenir. Petexbatun has given me a gift that will suffice for the rest of my life. And will I ever forget you, my chiclero companions, to whom I owe this adventure?

Without a word, Lisandro discards his rifle and takes up his machete again. Julio is grinning. Rey calls good-bye to the three vagabond monkeys and we resume our tortuous trek. It will soon take us to our pirogue, over there, close to the river.

We worked for three days to open a clearing, cutting down a small section of the dense tropical forest.

Here is one of the loveliest and the most spectacular of my discoveries—a heavy sculptured flagstone slab, 72 feet high, embedded at the top in a large pyramid. In the lower right-hand corner there is an even break, probably done deliberately to allow access to an inner chamber.

In turning the stela over we discovered a magnificent warrior holding a spear. On his chest is the symbol of the owl. The glyphs above his head enabled me to decipher the date of the monument: A.D. 738.

These three mysterious designs opposite the mouth of the figure in the first stela we turned over remind us of the curious number 333. Perhaps these designs are meant to illustrate his words. . . .

The calendar glyph for the magic day ahau *is given a prominent place amid the hieroglyphics, only a third of which have been deciphered.*

Our final discovery—an unfinished stairway. To the right are stone slabs hewn from the rocks. For centuries they have been waiting to be put in place, to form the fourth stair. Since the place where they were to be installed is marked out, everything points to the fact that activities in this Mayan city were suddenly interrupted.

This Mayan warrior is a prisoner. He is ligated to a hieroglyphic date by a piece of rope. He is my first discovery.

There are scarcely a hundred Lacandones scattered throughout the forests of the Chiapas. These last descendants of the ancient Mayans use horns to call their gods from the four corners of the earth to offer them copal.

One of Kayun's wives is preparing a dough of corn mixed with sweet cassava to make large cakes.

The rite of the flowered cross shown in the number 2 lineal at Yaxchilan is one of the finest bas-reliefs of the classical period. This relief was to help me in discovering the workings of the ancient Mayans' strange socioreligious organization.

Wise old Kayun, the most likable of all the Lacandones, is peacefully playing his flute, seated close to his young son. His canvas hammock, a symbol of wealth, came to him from the outside world.

Birds are brought down with an arrow that has a small, pointed antenna at its tip. Thus, if the arrow misses its prey, it doesn't have to remain lost in the branches.

PART TWO

XI

The World of the
Lacandons

A THICK fog shrouds the mountainous forest of Chiapas. Chilled by the early morning humidity, I am curled up in my hammock. To shiver with cold in the tropics, isn't that the limit? And yet I'm only two or, at the most, three hundred miles west of Petexbatun—actually a distance of five days by pirogue plus four days traveling on foot.

I had returned to the site of my discovery on two earlier occasions. I opened up a road between Dos Pozos and Lake Petexbatun in order to make sure that future archeological expeditions would have ready access to "my" ruins. It was then that an American geologist, employed by one of the big trusts, arrived in Petén. The local talk about my adventure had aroused his interest in Petexbatun. He offered to hire Rey and Julio as guides, but they declined. For a price, not in chicle but in gold, he finally got Lisandro to take him to Dos Pozos. The art treasures that I had scarcely begun to exhume fascinated him. And since, as he put it, I was working for an "unknown entity"—in other words, for no one—there was no need to show me any special consideration. But he would have to "discover" something on this site, almost anything, if he

wanted to interest the outside world. So he improperly re-
named my discovery Dos Pilas, "two troughs," instead of Dos
Pozos, two wells, which is what we actually found. But who
can argue with an American oil company? The site is now
called Dos Pilas. Petexbatun had presented me with a marvelous discovery but others robbed me of it. This, however,
is of secondary importance. I still cherish the memory of an
intensely vivid adventure.

And my companions in the adventure, what has become of
them? Julio, the peaceful Julio, is dead, killed in an *asunto de
mujer,* an affair of some kind with a woman. I could get no
additional details from the trapper who told me the terrible
story. As for Rey and Lisandro, they are hunting for chicle
along the borders of British Honduras.

This is my third visit to the Chiapas. Before making it, I had
lived for ten months among the Quiché Mayans of the Guatemalan highlands and for seven months among the Mayan
Indians of Yucatán. I was following my first hunch: that the
quest for an explanation of why the great Mayans of Petén
disappeared must be conducted in the Indian world of today.
The discovery of Dos Pozos definitely proved to me that the
most unbelievable surprises await anyone who attempts the
impossible. From then on the Mayan world appeared different. It had assumed a deeper significance and seemed somehow to come closer to its own inner realities.

This conviction was to induce me to try to determine the
real meaning of all the ethnographic data I had collected; it
was to impel me to continue along the path that might lead to
certain fundamental truths, truths that would in the end
enable me to discover and disclose for the first time the key to
the Mayan conundrum. And it was during my last sojourn in
the cold, damp fog-ridden forests of the Chiapas that everything was to begin.

My lodging consists of a simple roof made of palms hanging
from a series of large wooden stakes. It is at once an attic, a

chicken coop and a shed. To obtain living quarters here I offered the proprietor, Bor, my aluminum cup. I have missed it ever since but I have no regrets. I now drink from a calabash gourd, a receptacle less sturdy than metal but more pleasant to handle. I appreciate the hospitality of this Lacandon Indian and I even experience a certain happiness at being in touch with his universe, although it's very unfamiliar to me. Isolation makes a man more sensitive to human presence. What could be more moving than the daily sight of women and children in the hostile world that surrounds the forest! I am about three weeks' walking distance from the nearest civilized area. Bor's kingdom is limited to the four huts occupied by the numerous members of his family.

The Lacandon group, which is now reduced to about a hundred people, no longer lives as a tribe but rather in family units dispersed throughout this thick and humid jungle where heavy rains fall during eleven months of the year. A hundred individuals occupying a territory of six thousand square miles! Each *caribal* is separated from the next by a two- or three-day walk. (A caribal consists of a series of huts that shelter one family from the neighboring group.) Here you find absolute solitude, which helps to explain why the Lacandons are the only Indians in all of Central America that never succumbed to either Christian or Spanish influence.

I am inclined to identify myself with these semi-nomads. There is something indefinable, spellbinding, about them. Can it be that my adolescent dreams about the "noble savage," so dear to Jean-Jacques Rousseau, have come true here? But I have lived long enough among the Lacandons to know that the inner realities of this human society are far less idyllic than one might think.

It is to my passion for the Mayan world that I owe the rather touching life I am leading today. The Lacandons are considered to be the last descendants of the classical Mayans. This may seem an exaggeration, yet it is accepted by most Mayan specialists.

At the start of the present century, the Lacandons were included in the linguistic *Cohol* group, which used the tongue spoken today by the Chortis, in the region near the Honduras border. Specialists established this kinship on the basis of evidence supplied by a Cohol-Spanish grammar written by a Franciscan at Dolores in 1696. Dolores was the name the Spaniards gave to the last Lacandon village they conquered.

After this defeat, the members of the great Indian tribe decided to disperse in small groups to the depths of the forest of Chiapas to escape the yoke of the foreign aggressor. Actually, however, Dolores represented a total defeat for the Spaniards. Isolated in the heart of the forest, far from all means of communication, deserted by the local inhabitants, the victors found the place to be a veritable inferno, just like Tayasal in Petén. An expeditionary force against the Lacandons left the highlands of Guatemala at the same time as a similar force left Yucatán to fight the Itzas. This was probably a well planned and concerted operation. The Spanish garrison managed to survive in Dolores for almost a year. Then the forest took over the village. No Lacandon Indian ever returned to it. Today it is impossible to find the place where it was formerly located.

Since the Franciscan monk had written his grammar on that very site, it was assumed that he had obtained his information from a Lacandon. But in 1907, the ethnographer, Tozzer, showed that the Lacandons spoke a language identical with that of the Mayans of Yucatán.

In addition to the linguistic affinities and the fact that both peoples lived in an area that contained classical cities, two important points appear to confirm the theory that a very close kinship existed between the Lacandons and the ancient Mayans. There is the striking observation made by early explorers and later by ethnographers that the Lacandon Indians still worship gods in the ancient abandoned temples of the forest. In addition, there is an amazing resemblance between the features of the Lacandons and those of the ancient figures sculptured on the bas-reliefs, a resemblance that strikes me more and more with every passing day. Bor's son-in-law, for instance, looks as if he stepped directly out of a stela engraved a thousand years ago.

The smoke from Bor's large cigar disappears in the opaque morning fog. Preceded by his two young wives, he passes close to where I stand but he ignores me. In his ample, ankle-length white cotton tunic, he appears to have a certain majesty which his companions do not share. If you add the ages of his two young wives, the total comes to less than half the age of their patriarchal husband. The women are dressed and coiffed in the same manner as he. All Lacandons, men and women alike, wear their hair to their shoulders; long hair is thought to confer magical powers.

Bor's latest wife is not more than eleven years old. Her fifty-year-old husband allows her little freedom. He seems to be constantly at her side. During the initial part of my stay, I tended to feel sorry for the little girl. But I soon came to realize that I was reacting like a Westerner and that this child-wife would have laughed in my face had I evinced the slightest compassion. Actually, she adores her old husband and never gives him a moment's peace. She can be demanding, even tyrannical. It was she who urged him to come and beg me for a few of the paltry utensils that are part of my meager equipment. If she had her way, I would be stripped bare, without a hammock, blankets or notebook.

Bor accompanies her wherever she goes, not only in order to keep an eye on her, but also to protect her from vicious animals, snakes or potential rapists. The acquisition of women by any and every means is the principal preoccupation of the Lacandons. A woman represents a certain amount of working capital as well as a procreator. She is the most ardently coveted of all earthly goods and the hardest to obtain.

Dispersed since the fall of Dolores, the Lacandons have not managed to establish a community structure. With the collapse of the family as a unit, and the absence of any kind of

collective restraint, the masculine penchant for polygyny has
been given free rein. When two different Lacandon groups
meet, strange transactions take place. Even before their birth,
women and young girls are traded and contracts often made.
The most important part of every contract pertains to the
paramount question of women. Before contracts are signed,
delicate and occasionally quite dangerous arrangements have
to be made. For this reason contracts have become rare. With
a bit of luck, it may still be possible to witness the signing of
one of these documents.

During my first stay in the region, I settled on the banks of
the Lacantun River, in the caribal of Chankin. One night, Bor,
whom I did not know at that time, suddenly appeared from
behind a hut. In the dark, it was scarcely possible to distinguish his silhouette, but he was shouting to announce his
presence. The effect was so startling that the entire camp was
seized with panic. Chankin, tossing aside the bow and arrow
he usually used for hunting, leveled an old rifle which, by
some miracle, he had managed to snatch from its hiding place.
There then ensued an incredible shouting match between the
two men. Bor finally decided to emerge from the forest. He
walked toward us calmly. Realizing that my presence would
create a diversion, he soon began to inspect my belongings.
Then he crouched near my hearth. Late that night, without a
word, he entered Chankin's hut. An interminable discussion
followed. Later, I learned that he had asked for the hand of
my host's daughter, aged eight. The discussion went on until
midnight. Bor emerged alone and came to crouch beneath my
hammock where he proceeded to sing disconcerting chants for
hours on end. At dawn, he stood up like a spring uncoiling
itself, brushed the flat of his hand against his long tunic to
remove the dust and left without a comment or salutation. But
the discussion must have had a positive outcome: later I
learned that Bor's child-wife is one of Chankin's daughters.

In the first caribal at which I stayed, a big young fellow kept
his "own hearth." He was obviously not one of Chankin's sons.

A little girl of five brought him his food and served it with great care. This was no game! The two formed a couple! My host had presented this child to the adolescent boy with the understanding that she was to be one of his wives. Of course, the marriage would not be consummated until the little girl reached puberty, around the age of ten. In the meantime, she was doing quite well in her role of housekeeper. The young man, for his part, was obliged to live in his father-in-law's hut, although he ate apart. He stayed there many long years and helped with the farming. Far from complaining about this, he considered himself lucky. He had acquired a wife!

This particular aspect of Lacandon social life is very unlike the ancient customs of the Mayans. The old rule of exogamy that required a man to take his wife from a clan other than his own (each clan was designated by the name of an animal) no longer exists. For a man seeking a wife, authority, personal prestige and capacity to inspire fear are all-important assets. Any transaction involving the acquisition of a wife is taken very seriously. Refusal can result in the worst kinds of reprisals; it can even lead to criminal acts.

Thus, the more feared a man happens to be, the better is his chance of acquiring a wife. The more wives he has, the greater is his prestige and consequently the better are his chances of acquiring additional wives. This curious social situation enables certain elderly Lacandons to become the owners of many very young wives; the young men are often reduced to acquiring women who have been abandoned or are sterile.

Chankin's son-in-law was quite right to feel he was privileged. By what extraordinary means had he managed to drive such a good bargain? The deal could have been the consequence of an agreement made by Chankin with some other elderly owner of several wives who offered one of his own daughters in exchange for his son's acquisition of the little five-year-old. Such transactions are fairly common.

It is not difficult to imagine the scenes that occur when so many wives are acquired by a few fearsome patriarchs. Cajoled and spoiled by their parents, the children are little autocrats when they are young. But as soon as boys reach adolescence, their physical prowess is considered a threat to their father, who fears their rivalry. The young wives then become coveted objects and are watched over jealously. It is therefore best to get rid of the young wolf as soon as possible and by any available means. The adolescents usually leave the paternal caribal when they are very young. Before settling down in the forest, they often take with them their old mother whom the head of the caribal has abandoned.

All of this does not mean that life among the Lacandons is unpleasant. Quite the contrary! In time, these conjugal matters take care of themselves and cease to affect daily life. Sometimes the arrival of a stranger, viewed as an intrusion, tends to revive the husband's smoldering jealousy. I'm speaking of the arrival of a stranger who is also a Lacandon. A foreigner is an altogether different matter. He becomes an object of interest, especially if he is, like myself, a white man, bearded, staying only temporarily and the fortunate possessor of a bag containing aluminum plates, knives, a machete, a rifle and heaven knows what other treasures.

In half an hour, if it doesn't rain, the sun will dissipate the daily fog that shrouds these mountains. During the past two weeks the sun appeared only twice, each time at the same hour: eight o'clock in the morning.

A hovering cloud is breaking up at the edge of the forest. Good! We'll have fine weather today. The sky is clear, but Bor seems hardly to notice. He is returning with his two companions, his arms full of large lavender morning glories. Yesterday the three of them brought similar bouquets. The Mayans used to offer flowers to their gods. Do their most recent descendants observe the same rites? The narcotic seed called *oliuhqui*, already mentioned by the Spanish chroniclers as an instrument of magic, was the source of these lovely lavender *ipomoea*.

I hasten to catch up with my host. When I approach his hut I stop and stand stock still, completely taken aback. Bor and his two wives are crouching in the sun, devouring with obvious relish the large flowers, still moist with morning dew, that they had just gathered. Once again I had allowed my imagination to run away with me. I was thinking of a rite long since forgotten. What I am witnessing now is an alimentary custom, and a rather poetic one at that. Noting my surprise, Bor grins and offers me his last two flowers. Although they are perhaps slightly sweetish, I find them altogether tasteless.

The two women go into the hut. Bor, satiated, fashions an enormous cigar by rolling a large tobacco leaf on his thigh. He lights it with a twig from the fire and inhales the smoke with obvious pleasure. The day has scarcely begun, but this is already his second cigar. Cigar smoking doesn't seem to bother him despite the fact that the nicotine content is tremendous. The local tobacco, allowed to grow carelessly any which way in the corn fields, is not subject to any curing process. The leaves are merely hung from the roof to dry after the central vein has been removed. A garland of such leaves hangs above my hammock. In the caribal, the consumption of tobacco is considerable. Smoking is an ancestral custom. When the first tobacco leaves of the season appear, the Lacandons roll cigars which they light symbolically before offering them, with a prayer, to the sacred fires. There is no age limit for this essentially masculine activity. As soon as children can take a few steps of their own, they are presented with thick cigars and encouraged to smoke.

Bor is a great hunter. He takes down his bow for me to admire. Then he checks his collection of arrows, a precaution he takes every single day. Something is wrong with one of them. From a bundle of thin bamboo sticks hanging next to the tobacco leaves on the roof of his hut, he selects one strip. He examines it minutely. Not so good . . . From the dying fire under the open shed he takes an ember and rubs it against the defective spot on the bamboo. His object is to make sure that the arrow is sufficiently flexible. Then he holds it up. There! The shaft is ready. The feathers chosen for the arrow are two clipped parrot plumes, identical in size. Bor affixes the feathers to the shaft with a cotton thread dipped in wild beeswax. The main problem is to make sure that the two plumes are of equal weight, so that there will be no imbalance. Finally, he attaches the arrowhead.

I ply Bor with questions, using gestures and expressive looks. Certain of the arrows have flint arrowheads, and I am eager to ascertain what Bor does to shape them so delicately. At first he hesitates. I beg him again to tell me. At this point he gets up and goes into the hut. After a minute or so he emerges holding a magnificent flint node as well as a piece of animal horn that looks like the antler of a deer. In his left hand he is holding a big stone the size of my fist. Bor crouches and begins to scrape the edge of the flint with the stone. Having completed this task, he takes the piece of deer antler, holds it against the flint and hits it a sharp, quick blow with the stone. In other words, the piece of antler serves as a hammer. A piece of flint falls into the folds of his tunic. How marvelous! It has the exact shape of an arrowhead. I am fascinated by Bor's gestures, a heritage from another age. This archaic technique reminds me of man's entire prehistory. Yes! Without realizing it, this old Lacandon Indian has just offered me a living reminder of man's first gropings as he set out to conquer the universe.

Here, in this Mesoamerican land, a Paleolithic survival in the European sense of the term is out of the question. Man did not arrive on this continent until 20000 B.C. All the chronological data established by our prehistorians on the basis of stone tools discovered in the lowest geological strata have no significance in this context. Bor has just presented me with a striking illustration of this fact, for the technique he employed was derived from his Mayan ancestors. The Mayans presumably used the same technique when they sharpened their lances. Of course, they did not know about the bow and arrow, nor even about the dart or *atatl,* the typical weapon of the first Toltec invaders who descended on Yucatán in the eleventh century. The bow, used by the nomad hunters of the northern plains, made its appearance on the plains of Anáhuac in the twelfth century. It was introduced to the Mayans at the close of the thirteenth century by Mexican mercenaries summoned to Yucatán by the King of Mayapán, who hoped to settle certain territorial differences and thereby establish his hegemony over the entire area.

Yesterday, Bor promised to take me on a hunting expedition. He doesn't quite understand why I am so eager to see him take his bow and arrows along since I have a rifle. To persuade him, I say that I am counting on him to teach me how to make use of a bow and arrow. We will also take my twenty-two rifle which he is extremely eager to try out. He assures me that he knows how to use it and I for my part am ready to believe him. All these rugged men hereabouts are excellent shots. Any Lacandon worth his salt at one time or another owned, now owns or will some day own a rifle. As a piece of property, it is almost as valuable as a woman. Bor wouldn't hesitate to lend one of his wives to a caiman hunter or a passing chiclero in exchange for the use of a firearm.

Unfortunately for the Lacandons the problem of ammunition is insoluble. If you give a Lacandon a rifle and fifty shells, you can be sure the gun will be used once a day and that for fifty days he will return to the caribal with game. After that, the rifle is no good to him. A hunter may have to wait months, even years, before meeting someone who is carrying a rifle of the same make and who is willing to give him a few shells. Meanwhile, the gun, wedged under the hut between two palm leaves, deteriorates. In the end, so sorry is its condition that it will be impossible and even dangerous to fire. If you give a Lacandon a large number of shells, the result will nonetheless be the same. At first he will fire it two, three, five or more times for the sheer pleasure of using it. Feeling suddenly very rich, he will give some of the ammunition to one or more persons from whom he hopes to acquire a woman. He will make deals and bargains of all kinds, and very soon his store of shells will be exhausted. I have seen this happen more than once to Lacandons who have received rifles and shells from me.

The only way to obtain quick access to a caribal for a long stay is to promise the chief a gun and some shells. Imagine my surprise when I discovered that Chankin had six rifles, all of different makes! Each of them, however, was almost entirely unusable. Having gained his confidence, I was authorized to make an inventory of all the objects in his hut and under the palm leaf roof, which is where household treasures are hidden. There is no more interesting way to get to know the people you are living with than to list their possessions alphabetically in the manner of ethnographers. Each of Chankin's unusable rifles had a story of its own to tell. Who were the trappers, explorers or adventurers who had originally owned them? How had Chankin acquired them? At no time did he volunteer any information.

I am tracking Bor step by step. I admire the ease with which he threads his way through the tangled network of trees, avoiding obstacles. The forest is his home; he knows its very essence, the areas where one is likely to encounter game, the fruits and vegetables that the animals like best. Very rarely does he return to the caribal empty-handed.

A fat bundle of tobacco is tied to Bor's back secured by a small liana which he had readied before leaving. In this way he will have the pleasure of rolling as many cigars as he feels like smoking while we hunt. In his right hand he holds the bow and arrows. The Lacandons never use a quiver. One of the arrows, barbed at the tip, is used against monkeys. Another, which Bor topped a little while ago with a sharp flint, is to be used against other animals. A third is reserved for birds; it has a small hollowed reed bolt tipped with a tiny point. This is a hunter's trick: if the shot misses, the arrow does not remain caught in the branches or buried in the many parasitic plants that surround the trees, but falls back to the ground where it is easy to retrieve. Today, Bor did not take along any of the arrows used for killing fish; we shall not be needing them on this expedition.

A couple of parrots are chattering above us to our right. Bent half over, Bor comes closer to the tree where they are perched. He gets his bird-bolt arrow ready, then takes his bow, holding it horizontally. The arrow soars and pierces the head of a bird flying some distance to our left. A master shot! Both arrow and bird fall at the hunter's feet. He is pleased with his display of skill and satisfied with his take. Like the monkey, which is eaten boiled, the parrot is one of the Lacandons' favorite dishes. This surprises me. I had often been reduced to eating this bird and I know from experience that it is frequently very tough. But hunters can tell the age of any bird and they are careful to select only the very young.

The tremendous advantage of the bird-bolt is that it does not wound its victim. The bird's feathers are therefore never soaked with blood. And parrot feathers are prized; they are used for arrow shafts and for adornment at festivals.

Using lianas, Bor ties the parrot to his back. We resume our walk. After about ten minutes he stops and signals to me to come closer. He puts his bow and arrows on the ground and points up into a tree. I don't see a thing. Then he asks for my rifle. No sooner do I hand it to him than he shoulders it and fires. I hear something heavy fall. It's a superb hocco. My host, very proud of himself, bursts out laughing. He returns my rifle to me, picks up his bow and arrows and starts back on the path we had followed. I call to him, urging him to come back. Aren't we going to pick up this fine game? He starts laughing again harder than ever. Then he says laconically: "It's no good." Is that possible? The hocco, which is about the size of a fat hen, is one of the finest birds in this region. Apparently embarrassed by my insistence, Bor stops laughing. Then in a confused manner he tells me that these birds feed on the most toxic seeds and that I might be poisoned if I ate one. I am very skeptical, having eaten them in Petén throughout all the seasons of the year. And so I pick up the hocco and take it with me.

Once back in the caribal I'm impatient to check Bor's statement. Soon the bird is browning in my casserole. I eat it with relish although I cannot rid myself of a slight feeling of uneasiness.

Night falls, I haven't experienced the slightest discomfort or digestive upset. Bor lied to me. Can it be that the hocco is one of the Lacandons' food taboos? This seems altogether too difficult to ascertain and so I am inclined to drop the matter.

XII

Incense Clears Up an Enigma

IN SETTLING down here I disturbed the orderly arrangement of the caribal. My rectangular hut with its roof and the double layer of palms on all sides was formerly the kitchen. Now the women are obliged to carry on their important household duties in the main house, which is similar to my dwelling but somewhat larger and enclosed by bamboo walls which I have seen nowhere else—not at Chankin's house, at Kayun's, nor at any camp. Here, as in every other caribal, one finds an attic for corn, enclosed on three sides. There is also a sacred hut where incense burners are kept—a simple, small structure with the sides of the roof coming down low enough to serve as walls.

The sun is high in the sky. Bor's two young wives have joined a third, older woman, his first wife. Seated in the shade of a ramshackle shed, around a hearth made of three boulders, they are busy preparing the corn. The grain, which has been boiled for a long time in lime water (the lime is extracted from fresh water mollusks), has remained in the water overnight. Every morning around four o'clock I hear Bor's women washing the grain and then grinding it for at least two hours.

During the day the Lacandons feed mainly on *posole* and *pinole,* liquids consisting of water to which small amounts of corn paste have been added. The Lacandons drink enormous quantities of these liquids. Early in the morning they usually prefer tortillas; if they have worked hard during the day, they also eat them at night.

Today the work was hard. Bor returns from his corn field which he had been weeding since dawn. With light rhythmic taps, the women are flattening balls of cooked corn between their palms. Large round cakes are thus formed which the women place on a terra cotta slab suspended over the fire. In a few seconds the cakes are ready to be eaten; they are delicious when consumed while still hot. I am quite familiar with this kind of Indian bread, having eaten it for years in every Mayan region. It is one of the staples of the diet in Mexico. However, the Lacandons are the only ones who make such large tortillas, five or six times the size of most. Their tortillas also taste better because the women sweeten the corn paste with cassava. The first time I was offered cassava cooked in ashes I was taken by surprise. The descendants of the Mayans, the very first people to cultivate corn, apparently also fed on tuberous roots.

The Lacandons cultivate three kinds of root stocks: cassava, sweet potato and cabbage. Neither the Indians of Yucatán nor those of Guatemala engaged in the special kind of cultivation required to grow cassava; nor is it ever mentioned in accounts of the ancient Mayans. But books of the Chilam-Balam do allude to it.

The cultivation of sweet manioc, or cassava, is an interesting way of raising vegetables. All the forest peoples of South America feed on cassava. It is very easy to produce because it is grown by means of grafting. In any single area, it grows far more profusely than corn. Unfortunately, cassava requires eleven months to ripen whereas corn takes only four. On the other hand, cassava can be left in the ground for over a year. Thus, unlike corn, it constitutes a source of nourishment that increases in size without requiring any special care.

Cassava, however, is not the Lacandons' primary source of food. Of their vegetables, corn is the most widely grown, followed by black kidney beans and plants of the gourd family such as squash and pumpkin. Corn, beans and plants of the gourd family are the vegetables we associate with Mayan areas because they constitute the basic elements of the Indian diet. Like all who write about Mayans, I must underscore the fundamental role the cultivation of corn played in their civilization. One can even say, without the slightest risk of exaggeration, that the very existence of their great sacred cities depended on the raising of corn.

The cultivation of corn is a discovery that occurred on the high plains of Guatemala, in regions where the wild corn, *teosinte*, grows. Forerunner of the cultivated plant, teosinte served to transform the primitive, nomadic and hunting Mayan tribes into farmers attached to the land. This proved an important factor in the full flowering of their culture. We know—the history of all human societies bears this out—that agriculture, by making groups of people more sedentary, also enables them to make important collective contributions. Agriculture unites them in a common effort, insures a higher level of subsistence and encourages regroupings. These, in turn, lead to the emergence of population centers. We also know that urbanization promotes the kind of dynamism that is indispensable to progress and creativity.

A study of the Mayans reveals that their agriculture is a far cry from the classical type whose descriptions include references to such things as the advent of the plough, the tilling of the soil, the use of draft animals, etc. Paradoxically enough, the great Mayan innovators never advanced beyond the most archaic techniques such as planting over burnt ground (referred to colloquially as "slash and burn") or planting with dibbles. This remained true throughout their history. Every two years the Mayan peasant cut down large sections of the forest with hatchets made of polished stone. They burned trees and in this newly uncovered terrain planted seeds of corn

with dibbles, or pointed sticks. Inasmuch as they never tilled
the soil, the land became barren after two harvests.

In his corn field at the edge of the forest, Bor proceeds
exactly as did his remotest ancestors. The only difference is
that a machete acquired by barter has replaced the stone
hatchet.

In Yucatán, 500,000 Indians survive today by utilizing these
archaic methods.

This kind of prehistoric agriculture is characteristic of the
most isolated, the most economically and politically backward
ethnic groups. Yet by and large the Mayans were not poorly
organized. One may well wonder how crude techniques that
required so much time and effort, that discouraged large
numbers of people from remaining long in any one spot and
that served in the bargain to isolate the peasants could have
enabled the majestic stone cities to thrive.

Ever since my discovery in Petexbatun, I find myself pondering with increasing interest this aspect of the Mayan
puzzle. For a long time I have lived the life of the men who
raise corn in Yucatán and Guatemala, in the villages and the
milpas (burnt ground converted into corn fields). I have read
the relevant reports of agronomists and Mayan specialists.
Today, I am filled with admiration as I watch Bor's wives
shaping into cakes the corn extracted from the life-giving seed.
What I see disposes me to reconsider the Mayan phenomenon
in the light of such basic agricultural facts.

With remarkable continuity over a period of several millennia, the Mayans have lived on little hills in clusters of four to
six huts, isolated from each other by rather large stretches of
land (approximately ten to twenty acres). For every fifty
inhabitants, in some places for every hundred, there was a
meeting place for the celebration of religious rites. Religious
centers of varying sizes occupied areas of approximately fifteen
thousand acres. The population, widely dispersed, never
attained a high density: During prehistoric times, it equaled

that of Yucatán today—about twenty persons per square mile. Even the sizable religious city of Tikal, which occupies at least 250 acres, does not have a large population.

In each of the small ceremonial centers which constituted a rallying point for the several hamlets of a single region, there dwelt a privileged class of priests and noblemen whose living quarters adjacent to the temple were surrounded by marvelous permanent orchards. Here cocoa, a precious legal tender used for purposes of barter, calabashes of all kinds, fruit trees, sapodillas, papaw and alligator pear trees, yielded a great variety of food throughout the year. The further away one moved from these aristocratic agglomerations, the more the population thinned out.

In a symbolic way, the large religious centers unified the various farming groups whose members were scattered over a vast region. Periodically, on feast or market days, the peasants gathered in these centers. Coming from every part of the region, they crowded the vast esplanades which doubtless had been built originally for just such a purpose.

Unless one has lived among the Indians of the Guatemala highlands it is quite impossible to understand the fundamental importance of a center for religious ceremonies. Today the village, with its marketplace and its church, the latter usually built on the site of an ancient pre-Columbian temple, is the embodiment of this center. A good example is the village of Chichicastenango. In this community, which numbers only a hundred souls, thirty to forty thousand Quiché Mayans meet at certain specified times to attend important religious ceremonies. For the two million Indians of the country, the ceremonial center is really the heart of their society, the organ that provides the vital oxygen for everyone, the place where, for an immense number of people, the feeling of belonging is reinforced. Nowhere else does the Indian express so much loyalty to his religious obligations. Only here can he take pride in the elaborate feasts in which he always participates to a certain extent, no matter where he may happen to be.

In Yucatán the situation is practically identical. Because of the size of the area and the displacements that are required to bring burned land under cultivation, the large villages, created and controlled after the conquest by Spanish missionaries and later developed by the Mexican government, have always been assembly points, places of reunion. All the inhabitants of the scattered hamlets forming a single commune meet here at market time, either for religious celebrations or for political assemblies. These villages occupy the stable and immutable sites on which the great pre-Hispanic sacred villages of the Mayan ancestors were erected.

The peasants of Guatemala and Yucatán are first cousins of the ancient Mayans. By looking at them as living illustrations of an ancient past, we can imagine what these large central meeting places must have been like during classical times. It is quite logical to conclude that the Mayan cities were exclusively religious centers rather than places of habitation for urban people.

But the enigma still remains. The Mayans are the only historical people who have developed a great civilization based on a semi-nomadic, agricultural population. This in itself is unique and inexplicable.

But were the Mayans really semi-nomadic agriculturalists and nothing more? In the Guatemalan and Yucatán examples already cited, we should have emphasized too the important economic contributions made by traders and artisans to these native societies in the present as well as in the past. During the pre-Columbian era, the quetzal feathers and the cocoa from the Pacific lowlands brought great wealth to Guatemala. In the same period, Yucatán specialized in the production of native cotton and woven materials, large amounts of which were exported.

Nevertheless, four major questions have yet to be answered:

Why did the Mayans decide to settle in the most forbidding territory in Central America, where the land was not particularly favorable for the cultivation of corn?

Why did these highly talented innovators never attempt to improve their Neolithic agricultural methods?

How did they manage to obtain enough workers to build their holy cities?

And lastly, of course, what could have caused them to abandon so abruptly a region where they were so firmly entrenched?

Suddenly the forest grows lighter. Here is Kayun's caribal, not far from Bor's.

Curiously enough, it was modernization and the growth of the tourist trade that brought together these two owners of several women. A few crude landing fields were built in the wildest parts of the forest of Chiapas. In Petén a short strip of land had been cleared for planes because of the chicle. But here only a few woodsmen hunt chicle. Some of the big companies engaged in the research and development of valuable woods, especially cedar and mahogany, wanted to fly teams of specialized woodsmen to the Chiapas. These attempts to exploit the forest were quickly abandoned, however, and in the course of time the forest recovered its autonomy. But recently a handful of reckless pilots have agreed for a fat fee to land their small single engine four-passenger planes here for at least a few hours. Wealthy tourists seeking something new and authentic occasionally risk flying in a beat-up plane in order to see the great forest; they also hope to get a glimpse of some Lacandon Indians. The landing field is in a village called El Cedro. Even today El Cedro is the only place where these small planes can land.

What potential windfalls are in store for the Lacandons when this reflection of the outside world's affluence descends from the heavens! Stories are told in the camps about foreigners who occasionally offer knives, machetes, even gun shells. Suddenly, these people, who for four centuries had been living in isolation, feel themselves irresistibly drawn to the landing field as if it were a magnet—or a holy site of some

kind. In quick succession, five or six caribals suddenly
sprang up in the vicinity. But no others followed. Besides, the
new settlers are not permanently installed. In fact, the Lacandons never settle in any one camp for more than three or
four years. Nonetheless, what happened was an interesting
phenomenon—grist for the mill of sociologists.

I am surprised that Kayun was able to resist this kind of
fascination. I feel rather friendly toward this great old devil
with thinning hair, and I am happy to find myself once again
in his home, among his numerous progeny. He is older than
Bor but, like him, owns three wives, all of them very young.
He is extremely proud of them and seemingly not in the least
distrustful. I believe that he has now reached the age of
wisdom, that he has risen above concern for his status as an
owner of women.

I also value his unselfishness. I know from my own experience the feeling a visitor has when he first arrives among
strangers. Thinking of himself as the center of interest, he
expects people to react with warmth and spontaneity. So many
of our travel books are full of tales about friendliness readily
displayed and gifts unexpectedly given. But anyone who is
lucky enough to become deeply involved in a society that has
no written language will soon realize that gifts are not given
without the expectation of a gift in return, sometimes a more
valuable one. Any present of value, whether offered by a
member of the local tribe or by someone from a neighboring
one, awakens anxiety in the recipient; if he accepts it, he will
feel obliged to make a more extravagant one to the "generous
giver."

The foreigner, the white man, is looked upon as being an
individual so far removed from these established customs that
the question of reciprocity does not arise. He is merely an
object of curiosity and envy. Absolutely everyone will conspire
to extract the maximum from him. Intimidation, treachery,
false expressions of affection, flattery—all these as well as
other means will be employed. If none produces the desired

result, there is always the possibility of resorting to plain and unvarnished theft. I have very often been subjected to this kind of treatment, even among the Lacandons. Once I was even obliged to fight a man who wanted to take my flashlight by force because I had refused to give it to him. Afterwards, we laughed about it together. He claimed that what he had done was quite natural. He said: "Well, I had to try. . . ."

These men have amazing intuition. When a foreigner first comes into contact with an unknown people, he always experiences a certain emotion and occasionally feels quite uneasy. Sensing this, the natives immediately attempt to exploit it for their own purposes. This is precisely what happens to airborne travelers who suddenly descend into the heart of the jungle. Hearing the sound of an airplane engine, the native women rush to the landing field. Here is manna from heaven! But most of the tourists are not well prepared for such reception or for adventures of any kind. Very rare are those who thought of bringing presents to the Indians. And so you witness a sorry spectacle: the Lacandon women, usually so reserved, suddenly become demons. They fight over the flimsiest trinkets which the visitors, completely at a loss, feverishly ransack their bags to find. The Indian women try to tear these few things from the hands of the visitors and even attempt to take the rings off their fingers. As for the male visitors, they are stripped even more ruthlessly. Panic ensues. The visit, scheduled to last a few hours, is over in the space of a few minutes, to the great relief of the pilot. Wisely standing on the sidelines, he can think only of eluding the mosquitoes, collecting his fee as quickly as possible and spending it as he sees fit. Happily for all concerned, flights of this kind are rather rare.

When either flattery, intimidation or theft proves fruitless, the Lacandons resort to another technique—the offer of a gift. It takes time but usually turns out to be profitable, if my own experience and the tales told me by Chankin are any criteria.

During one of my many visits to Chankin's camp, he sent

one of his sons to offer me, "spontaneously," his bow and
arrows. Deciding to play the game out, I gave the boy my rifle
when I left. This is what Chankin had hoped for. Before my
departure I told Chankin that I had not been taken in. He
laughed heartily, believing his strategy was infallible, even
magical, since I, who knew him so well, had fallen for it.

"All right," I said, "but remember, the gun is for your son. I
want him to keep it because it really belongs to him."

It was my turn to burst out laughing when Chankin, taken
aback, stood there staring at me.

Things are different in my relations with Kayun. I made his
acquaintance during my first trip to the Chiapas, ten years
ago, when he lived on a different site. I had arrived at his
camp looking like a tramp, dead tired, starving and stripped of
all my possessions. He took me in, fed me and provided me
with enough food to last until I reached the banks of the
Usumacinta, where I had left my pirogue. To reciprocate, I
offered him my fine steel knife because he had admired it. His
reaction was entirely unexpected: no other Lacandon would
have behaved as he did. He refused the knife, saying with a
sigh: "You need it more than I do."

In the kind of emotional solitude experienced by any
trapper in difficulty—and such was my situation at that time—
I found Kayun's response deeply moving. Although the Lacandons know nothing about metal, they nonetheless can
assess the value of a knife at a glance. For them a sharp blade
represents not only sizable capital; it also confers a certain
status on its possessor. From that day onward, I thought of
Kayun as a benign father.

So here I am accompanied by Bor, in Kayun's caribal. The
head of the household, comfortably reclining in his hammock,
welcomes me with a broad grin. He had sent his son over to
tell us that he was very eager to have us come and see him. I
didn't know why. I had seen Kayun again after our first
meeting and had been able to thank him properly by giving

him a knife, a rifle and some shells. What does he want of me now? Is he having some sort of difficulty in which I can help him? I doubt it, judging by his broad smile. Well, then? Does he want me to come and live in his caribal again? No, it will be much better if I don't because of Nakin.

Nakin is one of Kayun's three young wives. When I saw her for the first time barely three weeks ago, I was struck by her gracefulness and her incomparable beauty. Gentle and soft, she performs her household duties with a perpetual smile on her face. I admired her from a distance but I could not allow myself more than that. But Nakin soon took an interest in me. She kept trying to meet me whenever she could and wherever I happened to be. I must confess that I was not indifferent to her presence. One evening, she approached my hammock, took my hand and proceeded to tell me that she was ready to follow me wherever I went. I was taken by surprise but also very pleased. For a moment I indulged in all kinds of dreams. I saw myself, accompanied by my lovely companion, walking through the forest toward the banks of the Usumacinta, a five-day trek from here. What a mad adventure that would be! But quickly I recovered my senses. How could I betray Kayun who had so genuinely befriended me? And Nakin would have to cope with enormous difficulties. Indeed, literally everything conspired to separate us. She hardly knew four words of Spanish. Her life was in the caribal with Kayun; mine was elsewhere, far from the edge of the forest. Even a brief affair would never do. In order to avoid further unpredictable situations, I decided then and there to leave the camp the very next morning. It was this decision that had brought me to Bor's camp.

Katun's perceptive eye had noted the beginnings of a secret romance between Nakin and me. It amused him a good deal and he never betrayed the slightest sign of jealousy. Did he realize why I had left his camp so hurriedly? I had the feeling that he was quite willing to give his consent to the burgeoning romance. Well, I will never reside there again.

Bor and I settle ourselves into a hammock next to Kayun's.

Kayun issues a few short commands. Nakin, obviously panicked, hurries off and returns, placing a calabash gourd filled with a thick bluish liquid in front of me. I am somewhat embarrassed. Laughing sympathetically, everyone in the camp makes jokes about it. Nakin and I, infected by the general gaiety, join in the laughter. This is all to the good. Each of us receives the same unidentifiable drink. I wet my lips. It is cocoa mixed with corn paste and diluted with water. Smelling strongly of vanilla, the drink pleases me. Then Kayun explains his invitation. He had wanted me to drink cocoa with him, in accordance with an ancient custom. I can't get anything more out of him. But the drink recalls to mind my Mayan preoccupation.

Etymologically, the word cocoa comes from the Nahuatl term *cocoatl*, which means "cocoa water" and gave us the word "chocolate." Cortez was the first to introduce cocoa to Europe. He tasted it for the first time at the court of Emperor Montezuma, who told him it was a "drink of the gods."

Cocoa is of Mayan origin. It does not grow on the plains of Anahuac. The Aztecs organized expeditions to the hot countries of Central America to bring back stocks of this commodity which became so precious that it was consumed only on special festive occasions. Moreover, the Mayan word for cocoa, *chacauhaa*, was borrowed by the Aztecs and "Nahuatlized" to become *cacohuatl*. Where did Kayun get his cocoa? Probably from the lowlands of the Usumacinta valley where a woodland cocoa (*Theobroma bicolor*), similar to the one encountered in Petén, grows abundantly.

Once again my adventures in this land served to complement the knowledge I had derived from voluminous reading. One day I was walking through an unfriendly hamlet in Quintana Roo. Nobody seemed willing to help me by exchanging provisions or telling me which road to take. However, some people in a hut did offer me cocoa. To be more exact, a calabash full of this liquid was forcibly thrust into my hands. I later learned that this was an obligatory ritual performed whenever a family suffered the loss of one of its members. Among the tribes of Guatemala, feast days, magico-religious ceremonies—in fact, all social occasions—are preceded by a ritual offering of cocoa. Each of the participants is obliged to drink it after having listened devoutly to the mythical but Christianized account of the plant's origins.

Spanish chroniclers of the sixteenth century like Las Casas, Landa and others allude to a feverish traffic in cocoa among the Mayans. The nuts of the cocoa tree even become a sort of legal tender in barter transactions. The nuts are never hoarded because sooner or later they will have to be used for the preparation of these holy drinks. The books of Chilam-Balam recount that only one member of the Xiu dynasty (founders of Uxmal) escaped massacre by the rival family, the Cocom. This lucky individual had just left the country to negotiate for the purchase of cocoa in Honduras. The first Mayan pirogues that Christopher Columbus spotted on the isle of Guanajo belonged to cocoa merchants. We also know that the price of a slave was fixed at one hundred grains of the cocoa plant. J. E. Thompson goes so far as to contend that the Mayans may have conceived their entire arithmetical system by learning to count the nuts on a cocoa tree. Mayan society even came to have a number of cocoa criminals. Landa described the method they employed: nuts were emptied and then filled with sand. The same author also describes in detail the festivals that the big cocoa proprietors were obliged to arrange in the month of *Moan*.

After the close of these religious ceremonies, no one was supposed to become intoxicated. This point deserves to be stressed because of its uniqueness in the annals of the Mayans. Unlike the Aztecs, who condemned to death any individual who was found to be inebriated, the Mayans were expected to keep drinking during the holy festivals until they lost consciousness or could no longer stand on their feet. This custom still persists in Guatemala.

Thomas Gage, the first English-speaking chronicler of New

Spain, a priest in the Mayan territories of Chiapas and Guatemala from 1625 to 1637, recounts with a certain relish the difficulties he encountered with the members of his flock because they insisted on drinking cocoa during mass. This carry-over of a pagan custom was so offensive to the Catholic clergy that the bishop of Chiapas finally forbade the consumption of cocoa in his diocese.

A millennium-old tradition regulated the attitude of the Mayans not only toward cocoa but toward trees in general. All our evidence confirms this fact, whether it comes from mythical tales, accounts of the conquest or ethnography. I remember an *x'men* (a sorcerer-priest of Yucatán) who respectfully asked a *baltse* tree (*Lonchocarpus longistylus Pittier*) for permission to remove fragments of bark from its trunk. He wanted to mix them with fermented wild honey in order to prepare an intoxicating ceremonial drink reputedly capable of producing rain. When a Mayan from Yucatán cuts down trees to prepare for the planting of corn, he first makes a series of offerings in order to elicit forgiveness for his brutal act.

In Yucatán, a traditional rule still enforced today specifies that any uncultivated land or any uninhabited house automatically becomes the property of the village community. On the other hand, all trees, including fruit-bearing ones, continue to be the property of the person who planted them, even if he left the country twenty years before.

One of the most coveted objects in the forest is the copal tree, which secretes a pungent sap used as incense. Copal has always figured as a principal offering in all the religious rites of Mesoamerican civilizations. Saps from other trees can also be used as incense. The best of these come from the Mayan forests. A hierarchy of saps was established and traces of this still exist today among the tribes of the Guatemalan plains. The most precious sap of all comes from the rubber tree, and in ancient times it was reserved for the most important rites. Prevalent in Petén, it enjoyed such magical renown that it was used to fashion the balls for that famous and holiest of games, pelote, mentioned by Mayan specialists as having been played throughout Central America from the very beginning of Mayan times. Nine kilos of virgin rubber were needed to make a single ball.

The Mayans had a monopoly of this essential commodity. It was so precious that they were probably tempted to add to its value by endowing it with a magico-religious imprimatur, a kind of sacred label guaranteeing its authenticity.

This brings us back to our central question: why did the Mayans settle in Petén? Why had they chosen this place of all places? It was covered with dense forests, very unsuitable for the growing of corn that constituted the staple of their diet.

If you consider the matter carefully, you can only conclude that the Mayans did not settle in this place in order to be engulfed by a hostile virgin forest but rather to become an integral part of a richly endowed region unique for its valuable raw materials. This is of course obvious. The Mayans did not settle in Petén in order to plant corn but rather to exploit the forest by extracting incense, a commodity that fetched a high price because it was used in religious ceremonies. The presence of the Mayans in the forest was therefore entirely understandable. By their prayers they sanctified the raw material which their huge theocratic organization so urgently needed. Every holy city that specialized in producing one particular commodity—whether cocoa or something else— presumably did so in order to export it for religious consumption. Some incense went to Yucatán, probably to Dzibalchén, the largest pre-Columbian city in the peninsula and only a few miles from the sea. It is the only city that shows signs of an occupation of more than 3000 years' duration. There is also evidence there of continuous contact with the classical Mayans of Petén. It should be added that some Mayans went in the opposite direction, to the highlands of Guatemala. The scenes painted on a vase at Chama, a border city on the upper Chixoy midway between the highlands and lowlands, clearly depict a commercial expedition. Many caravans also went to Kaminaljuyú in Guatemala, a city founded in the fourth century for commercial purposes by Teotihuacán emigrants.

The importance of incense (particularly copal) in the religious life of both ancient and present-day Mayans and the methodical exploitation of the sap are established facts. As early as the sixteenth century, Landa wrote: "They [the Mayans] cultivate trees yielding sap for incense which they use for their idols; they obtain it by cutting the bark of the trunk so that the sap can run out. The tree is big, shady, with many leaves . . ."

Oviedo, for his part, included the following passage in his description of the village of Sisimato in northeast Yucatán: "Over a two-league span there are leveled areas abounding with incense trees that are well cared for because there is profit in selling incense. It is sent all over the country to perfume the temples and oratories and to serve in the performance of sacrifices and mortuary rites. . . . There is no incense in all the land save here. To extract it, the natives make a hole in the tree the size of a fist; from this opening the liquid runs out little by little, coagulates and then is used as incense."

At Chichicastenango, among the Quiché Indians af Guatemala where I lived for six months, tons of incense are sold every Sunday in the market place. Transported on men's backs, the copal arrives from the distant lowlands of Petén. These Indians save 80 per cent of their budget to buy incense.

Kayun's invitation to drink cocoa has started me down a long road. . . . I now have an explanation for the presence of the Mayans in Petén. I also believe that they were able to build such imposing cities in part because of the economic resources of this region. My quest, nonetheless, still continues. But I very much doubt whether I will ever discover the key to their social organization, which was probably unique in the history of civilizations; nor do I entertain any hope of discovering why the large cities were abandoned and the people disappeared.

Nakin is offering me another cup of cocoa. Nakin, so lovely, so close to me now, yet so far from my present preoccupation. . . .

XIII

The Number Thirteen and the Sacred Round Calendar

I HAVE a friend. Her name is Nabor and she is Bor's first wife. It is not easy to tell how old she is—perhaps thirty, maybe fifty? In any case, she looks like an old woman and is regarded as such.

Contrary to what I had thought when I first came, she is a person who has a certain authority not only over Bor but also over the two young wives. She never forgets me when the others are eating tortillas or game, and she always intervenes when Bor, egged on by his youngest wife, tries to extort some utensil or other object from me. She even returned the small baking dish that Bor managed to get from me after several days of maneuvering. She sends me wood and water for my cooking, because I of course cook on my own fire, as is only proper, although I must confess that this system is not very convenient.

Is Nabor Nakin's mother or aunt? I am quite ready to believe that she is one or the other since this would explain her attitude toward me. Because her behavior goes counter to the interests of the caribal, it takes a certain amount of courage on her part to treat me as she does.

It is not difficult to understand why family relations are not easy to determine. There are no equivalents here for our concept of kinship, which define very precisely the position of each member of the family: father, son, cousin, uncle and so on. The kinship structures of the Lacandons differ from our own. In our family constellation, a father is always a father, the mother's brother is always an uncle. To identify the members of a family that has ethnic origins different from ours, a literal translation of terms should suffice. When you go to France, for example, you learn that *père* means "father," *oncle*, "uncle." There's no problem whatsoever.

But when one deals with people who have no written language, matters become more complex. After directly observing the people with whom I have lived for such a long time, I am told by a child the word he uses to designate his father. If I hear the same term used in another family of the same group and under the same circumstances, then I have the first link in the chain. In my notes I can then write opposite the word father its equivalent in the native tongue. But I soon realize that the same word is also used for other members of the family—for the mother's brother, for instance. My investigations lead me to conclude that in any given group, the child will regard his maternal uncle as his father. The ethnologist must have a good deal of patience as well as a profound understanding of the men he is studying to conduct successful research on kinship and the laws that govern them.

I have derived a good deal of useful information about this aspect of the life of the Lacandons from books by Jacques Soustelle and Tozzer. A work of Tozzer's published in 1907 states that the title of *yum* is bestowed on the father, the paternal uncle and the eldest son of the oldest uncle. One word alone is used to designate brothers, sisters and cousins.

Despite the usefulness of this information, I have not yet been able to determine how or whether Nabor and Nakin are related. I should have studied local kinship problems more methodically before coming here. But here I am, completely in

the dark about these two women yet feeling drawn toward
both of them. My friend is called Nabor, which means "House
of the Woman Who Distributes the Food." There is another
peculiarity of the Lacandon culture that complicates things:
the custom of giving people first names according to the order
of their birth. Thus, for example, the first son is called Kin,
which means "Sun," and the first daughter Nakin, or "House of
the Sun." The second son is named Kayun, "Singing God," and
the second daughter, Nakayun; the third son is called
Chankin, or "Little Sun," and the third daughter, Nachankin,
etc.

Until now I have concentrated on family names in the hope
of being able to clarify certain aspects of the ancient Lacandons' social organization. My object in so doing was to
learn something about the social organization of the ancient
Mayans. I was not the first to attempt this, and apparently my
efforts so far have been in vain. In one of his works, Tozzer
makes the following point: "Every branch of the family is
named after an animal and this name is handed down through
the males. The name of the animal may also be associated with
a particular region. The totem animal is called *yonen*, a
general term for all relatives." This, to be sure, was interesting
enough, but nonetheless very vague—exactly how vague I was
destined to realize later when dealing with the question of the
yonen.

Thirty years after Tozzer, Soustelle looked into this problem
more systematically and with greater technical skill. He discovered the existence of four clans in Indian society, each
possessing five different lines of descendants designated by the
names of animals. But this data was neither definitive nor
absolute.

What tricks the animal totems played on me! They cropped
up where I least expected to find them; they were nonexistent
where I had thought I would surely run into them. And what
chaos there is in everything the Lacandons tell you on the
subject!

At Chankin's house, the sight of his son frolicking around the caribal with a young peccary delighted me. Was the peccary soon to be devoured at a religious feast? The animal seemed so much at home with the child that I thought it was probably a totem animal. But Chankin said the peccary was merely his son's yonen.

"Yours, too," I said.

"No, not at all," Chankin assured me. "It truly belongs to my son. The animal protects him."

This custom of having an animal to protect you, a kind of guardian angel, is very widespread among the Tzeltales and Tzotziles of the Chiapas. They call the animals *nahuales*, maintaining that every individual from the moment of birth possesses one such animal although he does not know it. Its identity is revealed accidentally, through dreams or a chance encounter. The peccary of Chankin's son was therefore a nahual rather than an animal totem.

Because of my obvious interest in the animal, Chankin, who of course knew nothing about my investigations into totemic relationships, took me into his hut. In the rear, in a dark, damp corner, he showed me a variety of stuffed animals: a kinkajou, a coati and a white-headed monkey. He assured me that these were toys. I doubted that this was true.

As on every night, Bor, his three wives, his children and sons-in-law, are now all assembled around me. We are ready for our evening séance—recording chants on my tape recorder. The humidity has weakened the batteries; as a consequence the recordings are poor. But no matter. They should still prove a valuable source of information. Chants constitute important documentary material about any and every ethnic group. I still remember the many new and interesting facts I learned from the recorded chants of the Dayaks of Borneo. After my return to France, I played the tape back and translated the chants at my leisure.

In Bor's house I encountered a good deal of trouble at the

very outset. Nabor, that nice woman, was the first to offer her services. After a series of farcical interviews and amid general giggling, she resolutely approached the speaker and began to intone "her" chant in a quavering voice, as tradition required. It was an endless litany consisting of a single phrase constantly and monotonously reiterated. Once Nabor had volunteered, the other members of the caribal decided to do likewise. Soon the evenings were not long enough. Each participant wanted to record his or her voice and then play it back two and three times. These Lacandons would listen with unflagging fascination, their silences punctuated by excited comments and exclamations of sheer delight.

I shared wholeheartedly in the collective euphoria but carefully concealed my disappointment. The chants were of little interest or value; they shed no light whatsoever on the intricacies of communal life, the love life of the natives, their work in the fields or their religious practices.

The most interesting chant was the "Monkey Song," sung by Bor's second son-in-law, although the content was meager: "The monkey in the tree laughs and rubs its belly. In the tree the monkey laughs as it rubs its belly. As it rubs its belly, the monkey in the tree laughs," and so on.

Each Lacandon has his own song, and apparently it is the only one he knows. Bor, who had recorded a song two days earlier, announces with great fanfare that he has decided to "give" me another. The group forms a circle, impatient for him to begin and already prepared to applaud. The song's title is "The End of the World." He begins. The chant is entirely different from any of the previous ones. It describes a catastrophic torrential downpour in the forest that puts an end to all life. The audience is awed into silence, obviously moved. I play the song back in an atmosphere of profound but short-lived meditation. Soon laughing and joking gain the upper hand.

For the first time, Bor's young wife, egged on by her husband and Nabor, offers to interpret her chant, which she calls "The Wind." In a nasal voice, she begins to intone the monotonous chant, singing the same phrase over and over again. Finally the song is ended. It is late. Everyone goes off to bed. With great care I put the tapes back in their boxes and place the tape recorder in my bag. So far the machine has held up pretty well under all kinds of difficult circumstances. Many times, on a long hard walk in the forest, I would worry about it, especially in places where I was likely to lose my footing. The tape recorder cost me a good deal of additional strain. In swimming across the Lacantun River, for example, I had to hold it aloft over my head.

I return to my hammock, slide under the mosquito netting and begin to reflect on the events of the evening, particularly Bor's "End of the World" song. The title is a reminder of my main preoccupation, the abrupt disappearance of the Mayans. Do any of these chants contain important but hidden clues? Apparently not. You could scarcely dignify these monotonous, repetitive phrases with the term song, except of course for Bor's chant about the forest submerged by torrential rains. Each individual is very proud of his own special chant. Many years ago, Tozzer pointed out that every Lacandon has his or her own particular chant, which is related directly to the animal whose name their lineage bears. Fine. I have recorded chants about the monkey, the kid and the tiger. But what does the chant about the reed or the wind signify? Suddenly, a completely new thought occurs to me. It is the title of the chant that is important. I mutter to myself, "Oh, that's impossible!" I get up so quickly that my feet become entangled in mosquito netting. At last, there it is, my bag. . . . I take out the tapes and in the faint light produced by my flashlight I feverishly scan the titles I had attached to each box of tape. They suddenly take on a strange significance: serpent, crocodile, reed, monkey, kid, flower, house, wind—all the names of the ancient Mayans' Sacred Year! Resigned to spending a sleepless night, here I go again, involved in all the intricacies of the calendars!

When you first begin to examine Mayan calendars, you are disheartened by their complexity; but since they are so essential to an understanding of Mayan civilization, an attempt has to be made to unravel their mystery.

The Sacred Round—also called the Sacred Almanac, or *tzolkin*—was extremely important in the calendrical system. It is our rare good fortune to have the writings of the sixteenth-century Spanish chroniclers to lean on. Moreover, the Indian tribes in Guatemala use it even today. To my surprise, the exhaustive research I conducted on the subject proved fascinating.

The principle of the Sacred Round is in itself very simple. It postulates 260 days by combining a 20-day cycle—with each day bearing a different name—and a cycle of 13 successive days (from one to thirteen). The two cycles start at the same moment in time and run their course in parallel fashion for a period of thirteen months, or 260 days, until the number one again coincides with the first day of the first month, which is called *Imix*.

These are the names of the first months of their calendar:

FIRST MONTH	SECOND MONTH	THIRD MONTH
1 Imix	8 Imix	2 Imix
2 Ik	9 Ik	3 Ik
3 Akbal	10 Akbal	4 Akbal
4 Kan	11 Kan	5 Kan
5 Chichan	12 Chichan	6 Chichan
6 Chimi	13 Chimi	7 Chimi
7 Manik	1 Manik	8 Manik
8 Lamat	2 Lamat	9 Lamat
9 Muluc	3 Muluc	10 Muluc
10 Oc	4 Oc	11 Oc
11 Chuen	5 Chuen	12 Chuen
12 Eb	6 Eb	13 Eb
13 Ben	7 Ben	1 Ix

1 Ix	8 Ix	2 Men
2 Men	9 Men	etc.
3 Cib	10 Cib	
4 Caban	11 Caban	
5 Eznab	12 Eznab	
6 Canac	13 Canac	
7 Ahau	1 Ahau	

What is the significance of the Sacred Round? It has been investigated by many prominent researchers because the entire Mayan edifice was founded on it.

The German scholar, Schultze Jena holds that the Sacred Round was based on the fact that it takes nine lunar or synodical months for a woman to produce an infant. He therefore regards the number 260 as being "the oldest calendar figure directly inspired by observation of a woman's period of gestation." Although Schultze Jena knows that nine complete lunar months come to more than 260 days and that pregnancy lasts 280 days, he is not deterred by these facts. He simply cites a round figure—260—to make his thesis plausible. If we followed his reasoning to its logical conclusion, we would have to say that the calendar's essential figure is the number nine. But that doesn't happen to be true. The essential numbers in the Sacred Round, or tzolkin, are thirteen and twenty.

It is easy enough to explain the number twenty. We live in a world that uses the vigesimal system for purposes of computation and that represents man by the number twenty.

But what about the famous number thirteen? In Jena's own words, "the number thirteen is still the great unknown factor of the native calendar." How does he explain it? By dividing 260, the number of days in the Sacred Round, by 20. That's simple enough or rather too simple. Especially since the Mayans, in combining cycles, multiplied, added or subtracted, but never divided. Nonetheless, satisfied with his deduction, Schultze Jena adds: "Ingenious and resourceful was the mind that divided these two figures for the first time, using the quotient thirteen as the norm for a numerical sequence in which the figure twenty represented the cycle of days." I happen to be a great admirer of the books of Schultze Jena, but on this point I just can't believe my eyes. Like a magician, he has literally taken the famous Mayan figure thirteen and whisked it away! Because all his predecessors had failed to come up with an answer, he tackled the problem in reverse. He simply took the quotient thirteen and explained it in oversimplified, modern arithmetical terms. It is altogether obvious that this important number was not reached by accidentally dividing 260 by 20!

In spite of Jena's conviction that he had hit upon a clever answer, the problem still remains. As I have already pointed out, the number thirteen constitutes the basis of the Mayan edifice. Any analysis, any computation relating to that civilization, brings to the fore this fundamental question. The beginning of Mayan chronology includes the following notation: End of baktun 13. I was becoming obsessed by this number.

Endlessly, I pursued every possible lead. Since these numbers were a basic part of the Mayan calendars, the moon may have had something to do with them. I couldn't overlook this possibility since Schultze Jena did not hit upon the number nine haphazardly.

First, I addressed myself to the sources of our own superstitions which attribute a lucky or unlucky connotation to the number thirteen. It began with religious history. Thirteen people attended the Last Supper—Jesus and his twelve disciples. Among them was Judas, the traitor who betrayed Jesus. He was the thirteenth person, the bird of ill omen who changed the face of the world. His betrayal had occurred on the morning of the crucifixion, a Friday. Because he was the thirteenth disciple the number thirteen has a magical connotation even today, whether for good or evil. The fact that Jesus was accompanied by twelve disciples is certainly no accident.

I was also mindful of an ancient tradition observed on French market days, when eggs are sold thirteen to the dozen.

One thing led to another; I tracked down the sources and finally came to the Chaldeans. Here I found the first calendrical explanation of the number thirteen. The Chaldeans, having estimated that a solar year consists of twelve lunar months, divided their year accordingly. This is the origin of their duodecimal system. Since, however, a solar year actually comprises more than twelve lunar months, the discrepancy grew more marked as the years progressed. The Chaldeans decided to include an additional month every sixth year. Consequently, every six years there were thirteen lunar months. This injection of an additional element in the revolution of time was accomplished with great caution—magical and religious safeguards were resorted to—because it was deemed dangerous.

Aided by this additional and apparently fundamental information, I turned back to the Mayan calendars and the unexplained number thirteen. My working hypothesis proved a total failure.

Unlike the Chaldeans, the Mayans' tabulation of the lunar year did not result in a lunar calendar. I was trying to resolve a purely Mesoamerican problem with a Western approach. Consequently, I repeated, although in a different way, the mistake made by my illustrious predecessor, Jena. I now decided to review one by one all the known facts about every aspect of Mayan civilization. I would analyze the working of the calendars in an effort to apprehend the thought processes of those who used them. In effect, I would try to think like a Mayan.

Mustering my critical faculties, I would also probe other Mesoamerican civilizations that used the Sacred Round: those of the Toltecs, the Zapotecs, the Olmecs, the Mixtecs and the Aztecs. I would pass them all in review.

After embarking on this enterprise, I soon realized that the Sacred Round had survived all the cataclysms that descended upon the various Indian groups. It persists today not only in Guatemala and in the Chiapas but also in Veracruz. The only variable is the number twenty; otherwise the device and the manner of its use are everywhere identical. This key system plays a regulatory role throughout all of Mesoamerica.

Direct observation also revealed how very popular the Sacred Round is today. Every day for the last few millennia, magicians, soothsayers and medicine men (*Chuchkahua* in Guatemala, *x'men* in Yucatán) have used it to practice the art of divination and to tell sick people how to recover most rapidly. The Indians of the Guatemala highlands have given the Sacred Round the name of tzolkin. All of them rely on it.

Children are given the name of the day in the Sacred Round calendar on which their birth occurred. The twenty days of the tzolkin are named either after animals or after the elements and these titles reappear in the Lacandon chants. Each day is associated with a well-defined characteristic which everyone knows. For example, among the Quiché Mayans, the day called "dog" symbolizes sin, especially sexual impurity. A child born on that day will be called "dog" and will automatically be assumed to have the traits associated with that sacred day. If, as he matures, he proves to be chaste and pure, the people around him will nevertheless, perhaps unconsciously, attribute to him the traits associated with his name. Gradually and without realizing it, he will incline toward a life that is not in harmony with his nature but rather one that tallies with what society expects of him because of his name.

The day called "bird" is associated with good fortune in business. Throughout his life the child born under this sign will be encouraged by his family as well as by society to become a businessman. He will probably be successful because when people hear his name, they will feel sure that he was born for his occupation and that he has a talent for it. They will have full confidence in him and will be more than willing to do business with him.

To have a thorough knowledge of all the days of the Sacred Round calendar is to possess a sound psychological understanding of the society in which the calendar functions. The daily life of the ancient Mayans was governed by these name days. What role did they actually play? And how did it happen that the number thirteen, that mystifying figure, became the principal axis around which everything revolved?

Tonight, in the land of the Chiapas, the Lacandon chants have once again aroused my curiosity about these unanswered questions. When I discovered "my" ruins, I gained some insight into why the ancient Mayans settled in Petén. The Mayan lucky star shone down on me then. Will it smile on me once more?

XIV

The Sacred Drink—*Baltse*

THE lugubrious strains of a trumpet sound in the gathering dawn. Driven by curiosity, although I'm still sleepy, I jump out of my hammock. Behind my hut, near the edge of the corn fields, Bor, dressed in his long white tunic, is blowing his trumpet, turning successively in the four cardinal directions. He is summoning the gods from the four corners of the heavens. I stand a discreet distance away. He is picking up a calabash gourd filled with a liquid that looks like corn soup—the drink of the gods. He takes a long wooden spoon, which I had never before noticed among the Lacandon utensils, and tosses the offering toward "the four regions of the world." This is his first gift to the divine powers his trumpet call evoked. The scene has a certain solemnity.

Bor returns to his hut, which is also used as a temple. He comes out again holding a potbellied, white terra cotta incense burner, upon which is mounted the small face of a grimacing man. The eyes are flat and disproportionate. Among the Lacandons, this incense burner is an object of worship, an idol. Should a Lacondon require the help of one of his gods, he uses an incense burner that boasts the image of this particular god. In the bottom of the burner Bor places small wads of copal. He lights them with some tightly packed, slow-burning corn stalks. The incense burns. The thick odorous smoke soon spreads. This is the tobacco of the gods. Rhythmically waving a small broom made of palm leaves, Bor speeds the spread of the clouds of burning copal. All the divinities must have their share. I cannot understand the lengthy chant he addresses to his incense burner. Is he praying for something?

Bor is neither a priest nor a sorcerer—positions that do not exist among the Lacandons. But when the necessity arises of appealing to the higher powers, the chief of the caribal assumes such functions for a brief period. That is why every camp has its own small sacred hut to shelter the objects of worship.

Is Bor perhaps making excuses to the gods for the disturbances that for the past two days have marred the even tenor of his kingdom? The day before yesterday, Kin, Kayun's eldest son, paid me a visit. He is a healthy young man whom I like very much. He is attractive, alert and a keen observer. In addition, he has been helpful to me by supplying valuable information. He has often taken me on hunting expeditions and has explained the habits of various wild animals. He has also taught me a good deal about forest flowers and vegetation. When I am with him I have the feeling that the Lacandon world has become more accessible, that I can begin to see it in greater depth, that it no longer has that aura of the exotic with which I first endowed it.

Kin, then, was paying me a routine visit. I have no idea why this suddenly angered Bor. Bursting out of his hut and assuming a threatening air, he scolded the young man severely, going so far as to accuse him of taking advantage of the presence of a stranger to hang around his women. Bor was being unfair and this made Kin very angry. He grabbed a piece of wood that was lying on the ground, broke it in two and threw one piece at Bor, who caught it on the fly. Kin picked up the other half, and in a flash the two men were at each other hammer and tongs. A Lacandon duel! I quickly intervened to avert a disaster. I know all too well the inevitable, irreversible sequence of hatred and revenge that this kind of fight brings with it. Frequently, it culminates in a crime. But Kin paid no attention to me; he was trying to get at Bor's face. The old chief just barely managed to avoid some terrible blows. I pushed the two apart, rushed at Kin and struggled with him briefly, managing finally to subdue him and take away his wooden weapon. Exploiting his opportunity, Bor lunged at Kin, his stick raised, ready to strike. I planted myself squarely in front of him and stood there, whereupon he immediately quieted down. Laughing, I thanked the two men for providing me with an opportunity to get some badly needed exercise. I thought it best to urge Kin to return at once to his own camp.

"Come and see me tomorrow. But call out first from the edge of the forest and ask Bor's permission to enter his caribal."

Off he went without a word and Bor, grumbling, returned to his hut.

Calm, I thought, had been restored. But yesterday the winds of violence again shook the camp.

It was about nine in the morning when I heard the sounds of a struggle. One of Bor's daughters emerged from her father's hut, howling. There was blood on her face. I ran to help her but was too late; she had disappeared into the forest. Visibly agitated, Bor came out and stood at the doorway. He motioned to me to come over and hear what he had to say. His son-in-law had beat up his daughter in Bor's hut! Crouching in one corner and looking absolutely crazy, the son-in-law was sharpening his machete on a stone. His eyes were wild and his intentions were obvious. Although refusing to take sides, I stood over the young man and said to him: "You've beaten your wife and she is bleeding. You have no business to do that. But your affairs are none of my business. If Bor is to blame, it wouldn't be the first time. Settle the matter with him any way you want. But put away your machete. If you don't, I'll show you what it's like to be violent. And if you run away, Kayun and I will track you down as if we were hunting peccaries!"

Then I left, hoping that my threat would have a calming effect. Needless to say, I was terribly upset by these crises and by the tense atmosphere that now pervaded the place.

In violation of my principles, I had twice felt obliged to interfere in the personal affairs of the Lacandons. But what else could I do? Did I have the right to turn away from all this violence, which could easily have ended in tragedy, just to preserve my own peace of mind?

I take no credit for my actions. Fortunately, I am endowed with a powerful physique. The fact that I was a stranger also helped. Since the emotional difficulties of the Lacandons are none of my business, it was easy enough for me to intervene by a sudden act and thus relax an atmosphere charged with animosity. I had often had similar experiences with the chicleros. The only regrettable thing about it all was that I had destroyed my status as an objective observer. Well, too bad! The deed was done.

I blame baltse for all the violence. To judge by the quantities consumed during the past three days in the caribal, a most important religious occasion must be in the offing. For some time the toxic bark had been detached from the roof of the temple and put to marinate in a mixture of water and wild honey. I feel like cursing this baltse. Yet it interests me greatly. The sacred drink of the Mayans and consumed only by them, today it is drunk at all the magico-religious rites of Yucatán, a region where baltse trees are planted in village orchards. Here, in the forest of Chiapas, they grow wild. The bark is gathered with great pomp, and so is the wild forest honey, which is added to accelerate the process of fermentation. I myself don't like baltse. It tastes a little like sweetish licorice, which makes me sick to my stomach. But I am obliged of course to take a few swallows when offered some and to share in the men's drunkenness. (Women are not permitted to be present during the ceremonial drinking of baltse.) And this is just the beginning. Soon the moment will come when a great collective intoxication finally occurs; all the Lacandons will be rolling on the ground. Isn't it time to burn all these felled trees and plant rows of corn in their place? Yes, this is the period when large quantities of baltse are consumed, when everyone sings loudly and pays tribute to the gods. But then why don't the Lacandons paint their tunics with those large red designs of *achote* fruits as was the tradition during this phase in their agriculture? Is this ritual no longer observed? Be that as it may, the baltse is flowing amply in the caribal; it is making the men irritable and mean.

Bor is nearing the end of his incantations. He deposits his incense burner in the little sacred hut and emerges with two calabash gourds filled with baltse! And it's scarcely six o'clock in the morning! There's no way to avoid it. With false alacrity I accept the gourd he offers me and even ask him to roll one of his enormous cigars for me. What a breakfast!

My host's attitude toward me has changed. I have the feeling that I no longer represent for him an inexhaustible supplier of metal receptacles. And, of course, in this he is quite right: I have virtually none left. But that's something he doesn't know.

Contrary to what I had thought, my timely intervention in the personal affairs of the Lacandons was greatly appreciated. It served to restore the friendly relationship that had existed between the parties, and thereafter both sides evidenced a new and warmer feeling toward me. Bor now assures me that he has mentioned me to his gods, and his son-in-law, accompanied by his wife, comes to my hut to thank me. I am even asked to paint her face with Mercurochrome. For his part, Kin is glad to present me with a wild turkey.

"I killed it for you," he says laconically upon arriving at the caribal.

Then he makes an unexpected proposal: he will guide me to Yaxchilán!

"But look here, Kin, that's at least ten days walking for you, and I have nothing to offer in exchange for your services."

"I don't want a thing. I just want to accompany you. It's a long and difficult trip, and you shouldn't go alone. Kayun agrees with me. You must accept my offer because it was your physical strength that calmed my rage. You are like a brother."

Deeply moved, I accept this very unexpected proposal. As I swallow my baltse concoction I smile, thinking, God, how paradoxical life is! I have always felt great skepticism about the trivial melodramas that so often grow out of spontaneous friendships with woodsmen. And now this is happening to me! I return to my hammock, inhaling the fumes of Bor's fat cigar that I have had to relight three times.

I am on my fourth calabash gourd filled with baltse! The heat is stifling. The women are busy preparing the cocoa. It is becoming terribly difficult to take notes. Nearby, Bor is loquacious. I am anxious to make the most of the information he is giving me. To be sure, I prefer direct observation, but I have no choice. My departure is imminent. I have a date to meet Candelario at Yaxchilán on March 15. Twice this unusual woodsman has proved to me that I can trust him implicitly. On the fifteenth he'll be there with his pirogue, of that I am certain.

I have just now finished drinking my baltse. Immediately Nabor brings me an enormous calabash gourd filled with cocoa. Bor has already received his portion and is consuming it with great relish. The incredible quantities of liquid the Lacandons can put away never fail to astonish me. Of course, during the usual daily routine no one drinks baltse or any other fermented drink. The natives confine their drinking to quarts of *posole*. But Bor is correcting me.

"No, not posole, but *kayem*."

Kayem is the Mayan word for a mixture of water and corn paste. Posole comes from the Nahuatl word, *pozolli*. In

Mexico, the Spanish language has assimilated thousands of Nahuatl words. To these must be added three hundred words of Mayan origin. All this makes spoken Mexican-Spanish a highly colorful language that is further enriched by an unparalleled exoticism. The French language too has Frenchified certain terms like cocoa, chocolate, peanuts (*cacahuètes*) and tomatoes. On the other hand, the word tortilla—*kah* in Mayan —which in Mexico is used to designate a corn cake, is actually a Spanish word meaning "omelette." Its Nahuatl equivalent—*tlaxcalli*—is no longer used.

The Lacandons share with the Indians of Yucatán the traditional habit of drinking quarts of this tasteless mixture. The custom was probably handed down by the Mayans; kayem, after all, was their primary source of nourishment. The *comal*, an earthenware slab used for cooking corn cakes, has shown up quite recently in the Petén diggings.

One small rather technical detail about the Lacandons has always intrigued me: the women make no pottery, whereas in all the other Mayan regions and in all of Indian Mexico in general, this is essentially a woman's work. Here the idols, the comal, the receptacles, the terra cotta drums—all are made by men. The Lacandons have no lathes, which is understandable because the Mayans knew nothing about this device. Bor tells me that his fine drum is broken and that he has no intention of making another. Besides, he has never been willing to show me how he works with clay. I assume that making pottery is one of those activities reserved for certain special occasions and surrounded with magical precautions.

Bor, who has been kneeling in the dust, rises with dignity and nonchalantly returns to his hut. I hope he hasn't gone to get me some more baltse. After the cocoa I don't think I can drink another drop of anything. He comes back without any baltse, thank goodness, but with his hammock tucked under his arm. He hangs it up next to mine, and now we look like two wise men discussing the affairs of the world.

Bor is very proud of his hammock. But he never uses this practical, comfortable contraption to sleep in. In his eyes it is a sign of conspicuous consumption. Every night, like all his Lacandon brothers, he lies down on a pile of branches resting on four pegs that rise about a foot above the ground. To rid himself of the humidity and the mosquitoes, Bor lights a small fire under the bed. The hammock, which dates from the seventeenth century, will probably replace this crude bed someday, just as it has in Yucatán. The dream of all Lacandon Indians is to possess big "matrimonial" hammocks and huge mosquito nets.

Weaving—unlike pottery making—is the preserve of the women, who also harvest the cotton that grows in various parts of the caribal. In their diggings, archeologists have found remains of this Mesoamerican cotton, about which much ink has been spilled. The chromosomic properties of the New World cotton plant suggest that it must have been crossbred with its Asian counterpart.

Hereabouts the manner of weaving cotton has not changed in centuries. In the *Tro-Cortesiano* Codex you can see the goddess Ixchel weaving; the method she uses is in every way identical with the one employed today in the forests of Chiapas. Seated in the shade of her hut, Nabor spins and weaves exactly as her ancestors did a thousand years ago. A basket filled with the cotton she has harvested stands beside her, its contents ready to be spun. One end of her spindle stands in a calabash gourd. Approximately twelve inches long, it is a stiff shaft made of hard wood. Two inches below the tip of the spindle there is a small round terra cotta disc that serves both as counterweight and shuttlecock. Objects identical with this one have been found in the oldest excavated strata. A slight thrust of Nabor's nimble fingers sends the spindle back and forth in the woof.

I keep thinking about the jade gimlets, and all sorts of questions crowd my mind. Are the gimlets in any way con-

nected with the principle of the wheel? Is there perhaps some
ambiguity in the fact that whereas the weaving is done by the
women, the terra cotta disc is fashioned by the men?

Bor is swinging back and forth in his hammock, a com-
placent look on his face. I would like to take advantage of the
atmosphere of confidence that prevails at this moment between us. The time seems propitious to get him to talk about
the Lacandons' pilgrimages. But the subject is a delicate one.
The pilgrimages are religious in nature and always call for
absolute secrecy. They take place annually toward the end of
February, after a major baltse festival when the men burn the
fields that will later be planted with corn. No one knows
precisely where the Lacandons go on their pilgrimages. Each
caribal has its own special destination, unknown even to the
women, a mysterious place, a site reserved for Kanankar, god
of the forest. There is a taboo against entering this area with
any cutting tools or in the company of strangers.
I keep hoping that someday I will be able to penetrate this
sacred part of the forest, not only because I am curious about
the pilgrimages themselves, but also because the area reportedly contains a site with ancient structures dating from
early Mayan times. Neither Kayun, Chankin nor Bor know
anything about these hopes of mine. I have been careful to
keep them to myself for fear of arousing suspicion. I am
counting on some unpredictable circumstance, some chance
opportunity. . . . But Bor, I somehow feel, has guessed
what's on my mind. He seems very reluctant to perform the
rituals that traditionally accompany the consumption of baltse.
Is he waiting impatiently for me to leave the caribal before
downing enough of the sacred drink to make him fall down
unconscious? Is he waiting to leave for the sacred site until he
is no longer embarrassed by the presence of a stranger?
Well, time is running out and I might as well broach the
subject openly. The effect on him is startling! His face becomes frozen, impassive. He gets up, halts the swaying of the

hammock and silently heads for the hut that is used as a temple. Back he comes with a calabash gourd painted with red designs and holds it out to me. It is filled with baltse.

"Drink in honor of the gods," he says firmly.

His face is grave and stern. There he stands, in front of me, waiting for me to consume the contents of the gourd. When I have complied, he takes the calabash and returns to the temple. He comes back with two gourds filled to overflowing. He hands me one and puts the other to his lips. Again he says, "Drink in honor of the gods."

Tonight Bor is singing. Completely intoxicated, he has joined his gods. I too am drunk but silent. I think of Kayun, of Kin, of Nakin. How numerous are the disappointments, difficulties and joys that I have experienced among these forest people! My vision is blurred but I can distinguish the wrinkled, friendly face of Nabor as she approaches. She hands me another gourd filled with baltse!

"Drink," she says, "and think no more about all of us here, since you are leaving us."

XV

Bonampak Speaks

KIN'S light, silent tread, contrasting markedly with my heavy one, is admirably suited to the forest. A simple wicker bag hangs casually from his shoulders; it is all that he carries in the way of baggage. My own bag is heavy, weighed down by all my sound and picture equipment as well as the items needed for a lengthy stay in the forest. Although Kin offers to help me carry it, his words fail to carry conviction. I naturally refuse, knowing that the Lacandons are averse to carrying heavy packs at any time and that they particularly dislike carrying the belongings of a stranger.

We reach a clearing with two huts—Chankin's caribal. It is ringed by a wide river that has been artificially deflected from its course. In this I recognize the hand of Chankin. The proliferation of a thorny bush, the *acahual,* obliges the Lacandons to abandon their camp every three or four years. Once the acahual takes root, nothing, as the Indians know only too well, can prevent it from spreading. They have found no solution save flight to escape this vegetation, which they abhor. But Chankin understands all about cause and effect. As soon as the corn fields begin to become barren, the acahual appears, making its presence felt in the very center of the encampment. When the men return from the fields, seeds of this weed are stuck to the soles of their feet. As soon as they become aware of this, they wash their feet in the hope of preventing the thorny plant from proliferating. Many people fail to understand the reasons for these precautions. Also, it is delicate, not to say all but impossible, to ask a stranger to wash his feet before entering the caribal (the edge of the caribal is about three hundred feet from the huts). Chankin has therefore devised an ingenious method of coping with the problem. Whoever happens on his territory is forced to wade into the ever-flowing river, whose course he has deflected precisely for this reason.

Chankin is a very special breed of Lacandon. For a long time he lived far from his own people. During a span of about ten years he served as a solitary watchman of the city of Bonampak, whose ruins he haunted like a specter. Moreover, he is closely connected with the mad adventure that has made known to the world these absolutely unique Mayan temples.

Chankin is away. His wives are beside themselves. They all talk at once, insisting that Chankin is possessed by demons, that he has gone stark mad, that he completely neglects his corn fields. They say that maybe, if we're lucky, we'll run into him.

We are on our way. As we enter the forest we are amazed to find a wide opening like an avenue instead of the sinuous footpath we had anticipated. It extends for about three hundred feet and at the end of it we find Chankin, riding a mule —a picture I'm not likely to forget. He is smoking an enormous cigar and grinning. Where did he get the animal? We are three weeks away from the nearest Mexican village. Perhaps some expedition has passed this way and left the mule in his care. Perhaps the mule is a gift. . . .

"What are you doing with that beast in this place?" I ask in surprise.

"Look, I've got all this," he answers, gesturing toward his magnificent avenue. "Just look at it!"

And off he goes, capering around on his mule, his long tunic pulled up to his thighs, happy as a lark, although the mule seems loath to put up with him.

Three times he rides past us without so much as giving us a glance, his face tense, entirely absorbed by this new game and the difficulties created by his rebellious mount. Finally he halts before us but without deigning to dismount.

"There you are," he says, "you've seen all this for yourselves."

"All right, Chankin, but this avenue will give you a lot of work. You'll have to clear it every day. And how, may I ask, are you going to feed your mule?"

"But look here," he replies, "there's lots of *ramon* about."

These trees, to be sure, have the kind of leaves that are fine for horses and mules, but what a lot of work it is to collect them! Chankin has found another demon—his mount which seems to require all his attention. What sort of pride is it that eggs him on? Surely he is not attempting in this way to avenge history or the usual rules in villages beyond the forest. He knows nothing about either of these. They belong to a world of which he is totally ignorant. During the colonial period, the Spaniards had forbidden the Indians to ride saddle horses. This was a matter of prestige. Today, authorities in the Indian villages forbid all individuals in their communities to use this mode of transportation; this is a matter of pride.

Riding up and down like this on the green avenue, is the woodsman trying to make himself feel the equal of those who were insane enough to give him the mule? Or does he feel like the master of the universe as he sits astride his mount and rides through a wide avenue that leads nowhere?

Night has already fallen when we reach Bonampak.

I arrive at my rendezvous still vividly recollecting three men enamored of adventure, endlessly searching for some indeterminate goal until that day when the entire course of their lives was changed as a consequence of their contact with the land of the Mayans.

The first of these is Franz Blom, an American of Danish origin, an enormous drinker and great lover of the good life. He discovered the Chiapas after directing an expedition to the Gulf of Mexico for an American university. Settling down in the Chiapas, he spent years exploring the wild forest and ended up by becoming the friend, almost the father, of a group of Lacandon Indians. He died a few years ago in San Cristóbal de las Casas.

The names of the next two men, Carlos Frey and Giles Healey, are almost inseparable from the city of Bonampak. Legend has so completely taken over the story of Frey that it is almost impossible to reconstruct his mad adventure. The people directly concerned, the Lacondons themselves, carefully avoid mentioning his name.

Carlos Frey was a young American flyer who reportedly became a conscientious objector. At the close of the Second World War he refused to join the armed services, fled from an overly mechanized society and plunged into the jungles of Petén.

His purpose? To discover the free and simple life. This of course was a naive conception of realities in the tropics. His desire to return to an idyllic existence among the "noble savages" can probably be traced to the reading of an article in some periodical or other. Nonetheless, and in spite of chronic maladies and undernourishment, his experience turned out to be a rather good one. This blond northerner, his face covered with a thick red beard, became so intimately a part of the life of the Lacandons that he took a wife from among them. For two full years the strange exotic romanticism of this American survived all the vicissitudes of a semi-nomadic life in the virgin forest. He participated in the collective drunkenness on feast days, offered copal to the gods and observed the prescribed taboos when his wife was pregnant. In short, he gave himself entirely over to the habits and customs of the La-candon Indians.

Then, on two separate occasions, he happened to find himself alone with the women and children of his caribal. Each time all the men mysteriously disappeared. Frey re-garded this as a failure on his part rather than as an insult, but it upset his entire life, which had become a deliberately vegetative one. For months he kept bombarding his male companions with insidious questions. He wanted to know the reason for their prolonged absences. The quest for an answer became an obsession. Then, one evening, Chankin, his wife's brother, turned on him. Having consumed far too much baltse, Chankin suddenly asked Frey: "For goodness sakes, why are you so interested in our trips to Bonampak?"

He had said too much or too little. But the word was out: Bonampak! During the ensuing month, Frey learned that Bonampak was the name of a sacred place where ruined temples were being devoured by the encroaching vegetation. When the white man came to Yaxchilán and Palenque, the gods and the ancestors had sought refuge in Bonampak.

"We are certain of this," Chankin affirmed, "because their forms appear in the light of our torches on the inner walls of the temple, and always after we have made our offering of copal; you don't see anything when you first enter these stone chambers."

These revelations altered Frey's life. He became high-strung, brutal and never left his brother-in-law's side. He took advantage of every possible occasion to drink baltse with Chankin until, weary at last of the struggle, Chankin agreed to take him to Bonampak.

It was an extremely difficult trip. Hardly had they arrived when Chankin ran away, suddenly seized with anxiety about the consequences of his revelations.

And so Frey entered the ruined temples alone and saw nothing. But this city, buried in the heart of the forest, completely transformed him. He thought that it would bring him fame and, who knows, fortune as well. Thus, in the space of a few brief moments, he forgot his unique and incomparable experience among the Lacandons, his young Indian wife and, to boot, the disenchantment he had earlier felt for an over-mechanized society.

He returned to civilization and informed certain interested persons about his discovery. But all his efforts to capitalize on what he knew led to nought. The world he had scorned now scorned him. . . .

Two months later another lover of adventure, Giles Healey, appeared in the ruined city. He was more systematic, less romantic than his predecessor. For some time he had been living with a group of Lacandons in order to make a documentary film commissioned by an American firm. That was in 1946. In spite of the official nature and convenient conditions of his undertaking, it proved perilous. One must undergo an experience of this kind to appreciate how much nerve and obstinacy it takes to see such a project through. But Healey liked adventure and the Mayan civilization attracted him. In addition, he had the eye of a photographer as well as great curiosity about art.

And so he entered the famous temple of Bonampak, peered into its dark recesses and played his flashlight along the walls. What a surprise it turned out to be! Magnificent colored frescoes adorned the walls, but they were partly obscured by a coat of stalactic limestone. Herein lies the explanation of the mysterious apparitions Chankin had described. The eye must become accustomed to the inner darkness before it can detect the fabulous figures.

As if in a dream, Healey saw long processions of masked warriors, court scenes, prisoners kneeling before high priests, ready for the sacrifice, musicians blowing into heavy trumpets that looked so real he could almost sense their weight. On the walls around him he saw the pomp of lordly processions, scepters and tiaras sparkling with plumes of such bright colors they seemed to have been painted only yesterday. Weren't these unique frescoes full of messages for archeologists and art historians?

At the cost of a thousand complications, Healey took many slides of the masterpieces he had just discovered. Immediately afterward he left for civilization. His documentary evidence proved a veritable bombshell. His adventure was an enormous success!

As for Frey, he vegetated in Mexico. Three years passed. Finally, leading a Mexican expedition, he organized a return trip to Bonampak. Unfortunately, he never got there. He drowned in the Lacantun River along with one of his companions, just a few miles away from the caribal where his Lacandon friends lived. They still regarded him as one of their own and retained a feeling of great respect for him.

Thinking about the adventures of these two men, I relived my own experiences at Petexbatun and my discovery of Dos Pozos. I recalled the bitter disappointment of my first return to civilization. For me it is not difficult to imagine the emotional solitude of a man like Carlos Frey. He found himself back in a society that was indifferent to him and his adventures; no importance whatsoever was attached to his unique experience. I can also understand the joy of Giles Healey because I myself experienced the intoxicating sensation of wresting from oblivion treasures that have been lost for centuries. And I know the light-hearted feeling that comes when one returns to civilization, when faces light up at the sight of evidence so unexpectedly obtained.

This is my sixth trip to Bonampak.

On my first, Chankin was with me. We had come from his caribal, which was then located on the left bank of the Lacuntun River. For a moment we stopped in front of a small knoll where Chankin simply said: "That's Frey."

The temple we first visited seemed insignificant despite the fact that it was forty-five feet long. Its facade into which three different doors had been cut, supported a roof topped by giant grasses that covered the entire edifice. Chankin held a lighted torch made of resinous wood—my flashlight had given out long before—and I followed him into the first chamber. Although the smoke from the homemade torch was suffocating, I managed nonetheless to discern a procession of imposing figures. By the light of our flickering flame they seemed like ghosts in colored robes. It was an unforgettable sight. The very presence of Chankin lent a striking reality to the murals. There he was, his hair tumbling to his shoulders, brandishing the torch that now and then illuminated his own magnificent Mayan profile.

These Bonampak frescoes—the Mayan term for them may be translated as "painted walls"—are quite justifiably considered to be one of the world's greatest art treasures. They represent an entirely new element for researchers in the field of Mayan studies. There is no hieroglyphic writing here, nor is there, unlike Mayan sculptures and bas-reliefs, any significant symbolism. These are simply scenes depicting the social life of a people, portrayed with great ease and finesse—or so it seems.

Upon a layer of white plaster whose thickness varies from mural to mural, the artist first outlined the human figures with a pale red line. Then he used all the colors derived from vegetables and minerals: blue, black, green, yellow, red. A good deal of skill in the use of color is evident, although the depiction of important phases of the community's social life lacks perspective and chiaroscuro.

The chiefs in all their finery, the dancers wearing strange holy masks and the lively musicians—all to be seen in a portion of the murals—constitute a feast for art lovers. The fact that they are partly covered with layers of plaster coating makes it difficult to decipher them. However, after centuries of humidity and water seepage, some of this protective coating did wear off. Fortunately, many scientific expeditions were sent off to Bonampak after the initial discoveries were made known. Specialists copied the paintings and Mexican archeo-

logical organizations completely reconstituted the temple and
all the frescoes for their own national museum. A little later,
the Mexican school of archeology and history undertook to
restore the murals. A small landing field for aircraft was
constructed near the site. Researchers from the Carnegie Insti-
tution published an excellent monograph, that contains superb
illustrations, on the frescoes. Thus I could examine the murals
at my leisure. Paradoxically, I concentrated mainly on the
sculptured lintels and stelae during my subsequent trips to
Bonampak. Most of these sculptures depict warrior chiefs in
the act of taking prisoners or brandishing heavy lances. The
chiefs are portrayed as they felled their enemies, and through
them the viewer is able to get a vivid, naturalistic sense of the
atmosphere of those times.

We have pitched our camp less than six hundred feet from
the temples. Kin is busy building a fire. I lie down on my
hammock. Directly behind me are the sumptuous frescoes that
depict a slice of Mayan life, something the sculptures do
not do.

These paintings familiarize us with the intimate and ceremonial life of the great priest-kings and the people who
surrounded them. We notice, for example, that women played
an important part in this society. In the second chamber the
scenes depict Mayan warriors attacking unarmed people
clothed in simple loincloths—ordinary people, probably
peasants; their skins are very swarthy but their features are
typically Mayan. The warriors are seizing them by the hair,
indicating thereby that from now on these people are their
prisoners. It is a picture story of an organized raid whose
significance becomes plainer when we look at the northern
wall of the chamber.

There we see prisoners whose fingers have been pierced for
the first blood sacrifice. Crouching, terrified, there they are,
exposed to the watchful eye of the richly gowned chiefs who
stand over them from the heights of their daises. At the feet of

one important notable lies the body of a victim; nearby a freshly severed head rests on a bed of leaves. These are human sacrifices—a far cry from the image so often painted of the peaceful Mayans!

Can it be that the ancient inhabitants of Bonampak were more vengeful, more bloodthirsty than their brothers on the other side of the Usumacinta? Is it possible that these Mayans were subjected to foreign influences?

This temple filled with frescoes was built around the year 800 A.D. The scenes painted here, therefore, reflect the life of those times or of a period just before.

At precisely this moment the great theocratic and pacific civilization of Teotihuacan was collapsing in the north. A great consumer of offerings, it did not permit human sacrifices. In this it contrasted markedly with the barbarians who burned the city, those precursors of the huge Toltec hordes that swept over Mexico shortly thereafter. The destroyers of Teotihuacan heralded the start of a new order dominated by warriors whose religious life centered on human sacrifice.

The frescoes of Bonampak attest to the fact that during the ninth century the influence of the new order had already made itself felt in this region of the Chiapas. Its quick acceptance throughout the Mexican territory was automatically to terminate the consumption of non-bloody offerings, such as rubber and copal. Thereafter sacrifices consisted of human hearts, still warm and palpitating with life. Regions such as Petén, that had been the source of the non-bloody offerings, apparently experienced a serious economic recession as a consequence of the change. This in turn must have generated internal disturbances whose eloquent traces I discovered in Dos Pozos.

Such deductions may seem immoderate, coming as they do from a Westerner who is no specialist in the field. But they will seem plausible to a pre-Columbian Mesoamerican Indian. We must not forget that for the Nahuatl invaders who overran Mexico, human sacrifice constituted the whole purpose of existence. Aztec civilization was founded on the need to offer an ever-increasing number of human hearts to the gods. The sacrificial stones in front of the temples of ancient Mexico were permanently bathed in human blood. The first annual tribute that these terrible warriors exacted from the peoples they vanquished consisted of young men earmarked for ceremonial sacrifice; their number was fixed once and for all. To inaugurate the great temple of their capital, Tenochtitlán, the Aztecs cut the throats of 20,000 people in the space of four days. Gone were the days when copal represented an appropriate offering to the gods. Besides, literally tons and tons of it would have been needed.

It is true, of course, that these Aztec excesses occurred long after the Mayans disappeared from Petén. But they are quite illustrative of the new order that was established immediately after the fall of Teotihuacan.

The entire religious life of the Toltecs, the predecessors of the Aztecs, centered on this ritualistic bloodletting. The famous city of Chichén-Itzá, erected by these invaders, offers a realistic image of this fact with its *tzompantli*, the "Terrace of Cadavers." Here the craniums of those who had been sacrificed rolled to the bottom of the large pyramid's staircase and formed a huge heap.

By the start of the tenth century, this macabre custom had become so important in the religious life of the people that when King Ce-Acatl-Quetzalcoatl refused to allow human sacrifices, he lost his throne at Tula.

The fall of Teotihuacan and the inauguration of human sacrifices apparently convulsed the entire Mayan economy during classical times. A damaging instability resulted that was to affect the entire territory. It must be added, of course, that other influential factors must have also intervened in order to cause a civilization as highly developed and organized as that of the Mayans to fall.

At this point in my reflections, amid the silent ruins of Bonampak, sleep overtakes me.

XVI

The Division of the Universe into Four Parts

THE green waters of Usumacinta sparkle in the bright daylight. Wordlessly, Kin contemplates the spectacle of this jade-colored river that flows with muffled force. There's not a tree, not a shadow above the vast stretches where the sun at last reigns.

Whenever I come upon a river after a long stay in the forest, I feel a delightful, dizzying sense of well-being that reminds me a little of the pleasurable anticipation I experience at the start of a vacation. Clouds of mosquitoes, attracted by the abundance of the sun, quickly recall me to the realities of the tropics. The Usumacinta! A river that seems powerful enough to prevent the profuse vegetation of the region from inching closer to its banks; a river that can mercilessly sweep away any tree big enough to disturb its eternal communication with the heavens. But how much time has elapsed since the splendor of those days when the Usumacinta was the Nile or the Euphrates of the Mayans!

Kin grabs my arm and points to something downstream. A pirogue is lying on the solitary banks. As we approach, my companion gradually slows his pace and lets me take the lead.

It's not the high, abrasive grasses that bother him but an apprehension typical of all men of his race when they near a stranger. And someone is definitely there, squatting before a fire on which two fine-looking fish are cooking. Candelario! Without a word, Kin quickens his pace and draws alongside of me. He and Candelario regard each other with a slight air of suspicion. But hunger cuts short this first awkward encounter; the three of us are soon devouring with pleasure the delicious meat of the cooked fish.

Kin is interested in Candelario's method of fishing. Candelario, for his part, is very proud to show Kin his bamboo harpoon. Kin then demonstrates how to kill fish with a bow and arrow. There in the pirogue are the two of them, exchanging information about how to fish. Each wants to try out the other's method.

As for me, I am thinking only of the "Place with the Green Stone" at Yaxchilán, quite near here, on the banks of the river. Kin has decided not to set foot in this ancient holy city of his ancestors. Is he swayed by fear of its magical powers? We agree that we will go there by pirogue and that I will get out while the two of them go off together to harpoon a few fish.

I am alone in the silent ruins. An abundant vegetation conceals all the monuments, making them absolutely invisible from the banks of the Usumacinta.

This is my second rendezvous in Yaxchilán. I carry with me the memory of the very extraordinary men whose lives and writings have uncovered the path that leads to the dead Mayan cities.

First there was Désiré Charnay, a picturesque explorer of the mid-nineteenth century. He was endowed with a prodigious intuition about the various enigmas posed by the Indian civilization of Mexico. The first to claim categorically that the mythical city of Tollan, described in Indian legends, actually existed at Tula in northern Mexico, he also insisted that its builders had likewise erected Chichén-Itzá, over one thousand miles away. His thesis was ridiculed by every single specialist save one—the German scholar Seler. Eighty years later Charnay's theory was definitely confirmed by some archeological diggings.

It is to Désiré Charnay that we owe the first descriptions of the Lacandons, some of whom he had contacted in Yaxchilán. Here, too, a most unexpected encounter awaited him: he met an Englishman, Alfred Maudslay. Imagine the surprise of both men! In those days it took literally months of dangerous travel to reach the region. Maudslay was the first to lay the foundations for a scientific study of the Mayans. His work proved a precious aid to all later researchers.

Another picturesque figure, Teoberto Maler, left his imprint on the city. It was Maler who named the city Yaxchilán. Earlier, Maudslay had baptized it *Menche,* which means "green tree."

Maler was an Austrian officer who had belonged to the entourage of the unhappy Emperor Maximilian of Mexico. Visiting the Mayan land as a curious amateur, he, like so many others, ended up by becoming deeply attached to it. Having noted with distress the sorry state of the monuments, he decided to save them from oblivion by photographing them. To carry out his resolve, he valiantly suffered heavy rains, solitude, malaria, malnutrition, forced marches, mutinies, desertions by guides—all the innumerable and unpredictable hazards of the forest. In order to save time, and aided by remarkable powers of endurance, he undertook expeditions in the midst of the rainy season, a far more difficult time for such enterprises than the dry season.

So perfect are Maler's photographs that even today they are used by archeologists to illustrate their works. Because of my own experience, I can appreciate the fantastic technical difficulties he must have encountered. A single slide sometimes took him several hours. Trees had to be felled before he could take pictures from a sufficient distance. Stelae had to be stood upright and platforms built in order to photograph certain objects at the proper level.

On the facade of the principal temple of Yaxchilán, a

skylight crest that resembles a diadem of open work masonry
served to give balance to the proportions of the edifice. Such
illusory flight is characteristic of Mayan architecture. Fortunately easy to construct, these *cresterias* added a new di-
mension to the monuments. They enabled the architects to
respect the immutable norms that were mandatory because of
the nature of the temples' interiors. In addition, the cresterias
lent a feeling of lightness and thrust to the edifices which they
had never had before.

I waste little time contemplating the sanctuary itself because a statue in front of the facade interests me far more. It
represents a life-size decapitated figure of a man, seated with
his legs crossed under him. His general appearance is reminiscent of the Leprous King of the Khmer temple at Angkor Wat
in Cambodia. I know this Mayan figure very well. He symbolizes the meeting point, the link, between past and present.
The Lacandons call him *Atsibilan*, "He Who Sets the Sun,"
and regard him as the head of a long line of ancestors who
reside in these parts.

Only a few years ago Yaxchilán was still a forest region to
which the Lacandons traditionally traveled to make offerings
to Atsibilan and his entourage. Within the ruined city Désiré
Charnay encountered Indians who were just terminating their
ceremonies. Recently, it seems, the site had lost its magical
and religious aura. But Kin's categorical refusal to accompany
me here suggests that some traces of this aura still persist.

Here I am, in front of a little temple which houses an object
that I regard as the most beautiful of all Mayan works of art.
But how difficult it is to contemplate fully! I have to lie on my
back and look up at the small bas-relief for a long time before
I can see it properly. It depicts two figures facing one another.
Each is holding out to the other an identical cross made of
flowers. Scenes of a similar nature can also be seen at Palenque or Piedras Negras, but I find the style less moving. In
all these sculptures the figures always hold identical emblems.

From this I naturally conclude that the bas-reliefs illustrate a rite shared by all the Mayans. Or can it be that they signify certain occult powers? Or the transmission of a mandate?

For a moment I think I have hit upon the explanation. I remember that each year among the Quiché Mayans of Guatemala, the civil and religious chiefs symbolically hand over their responsibilities to the newly elected officials. The latter receive a *vara*—a long staff decorated with chiseled silver, the emblem of their power. But the newly-elected chiefs offer their predecessors nothing in return. However, after further reflection, I decide that this ethnographical information hardly serves to clarify the scene depicted on the lintel of Yaxchilán.

And so I stare at it again. The scene plainly describes an exchange, or possibly a presentation, of emblems. The two men are gazing at one another and their insignia are identical. Can it be that both perform the same function and possess the same title? On this bas-relief, as on all others of the same kind, the figure at the left is smaller than the one on the right. This is an interesting detail because it occurs so often on similar sculptures. Obviously, the artist deliberately intended it that way. There is nothing accidental about it.

What is the meaning of the flowering cross, offered with arms extended? Are the flowers in some way related to the renewal of vegetation? Do they represent the sun? The cross, however, presents no problem. It is the typical image of the Mayan religious world which is divided into four parts. Each of the poles represents a cardinal point. This division of space is totally unconnected with the magnetic north; rather, it is determined by the point where the sun rises and sets during the summer and winter solstices.

The Mayans conceived of the world as having thirteen heavens arranged in tiers. Each tier or layer had its own divinity. The heavens were held together by four brother-gods, standing at the four cardinal points. Beneath them spread the nine underworlds, governed by the nine Lords of the Night. Each cardinal point was marked by its own color: red for the

east, white for the north, black for the west, yellow for the
south. Everything in life had its assigned place in this space
and took on the color of the point where it happened to
occur.

The Mayans applied this primordial principle to absolutely
everything, including their calendrics. The fifty-two-year cycle
(the union of the Sacred Round with the Calendar Round),
which could be thought of as circular, was actually part of this
fourfold division of the world. Thus the years were distributed
to the four corners of the earth. Each new solar year, represented by a god or a number, was located at one of the four
poles; needless to say, its symbol differed from the god or the
number of the preceding year. The year therefore automatically assumed a certain color and aspect, either good or evil,
depending upon its location. A fifty-two-year cycle was thus
symbolically established, each year at the four corners of the
earth in separate accumulations of thirteen years. This gives us
the following pattern:

13 years   13 years

13 years   13 years

52 years in all.

Such a fourfold division of the universe holds many surprises for us. For instance, there is every reason to believe that
the entire social organization of the Mayans was based on this
principle; yet no one has ever studied this aspect of the subject.

Isn't it probable that the four clans of Lacandons described by Soustelle were originally determined by these four
symbolic points? And wasn't the figure thirteen, that famous
and mysterious number in the Sacred Round Calendar that
crops up everywhere, used to compute with exactitude each
clan's line of descendants? Each of the principal heroes of the
Popol-Vuh has a number before his name. Might not this

number refer to the line of ancestors from which he was descended? In the *Annals of the Cakchiquel,* several lines of descendants as well as their corresponding numbers have been identified by M. S. Edmondson.

In my attempt to understand the reasons why the Mayans had chosen the number thirteen for their Sacred Round Calendar, I went astray by seeking the answer elsewhere than in Mayan civilization itself. But I must admit that in the course of my efforts to resolve the enigma of their social organization, I had come to find the different examples drawn from various parts of the world extremely intriguing.

The well-known anthropologist, Hocart, tells us that the Massai use different colors to mark the four cardinal points and that they adapt their social organization to this principle by dividing the community first into two groups, red and black, and then into two subgroups, so that each quarter can be given the color and insignia of one of the four points. This type of arrangement immediately takes us back to the Mayans.

And didn't I myself, during my investigations in Bali, reveal the major importance of the Nawa-sanga, an image of the division of the world into four parts in which each cardinal point has its own color, its own number and its own magical word? Here almost certainly we find the influence of India. Besides, in Hindu societies the castes are distributed symbolically to the four cardinal points where the rulers reign. If I proceed just a little farther I'll find myself looking for the Hindu origin of our present-day deck of cards. Isn't it true that a deck of cards consists of fifty-two cards divided into four suits of thirteen each? There are two red suits: hearts and diamonds, and two black suits: clubs and spades. Is this a digression? Perhaps it is. I also see the explanation for the joker, the extra card that can be used for anything in the course of a game and that also rates as the highest card in the deck. According to tradition in India, above the rulers of the castes there is a superior sovereign.

I have no intention of becoming involved in digressions

about the diffusionist theory of civilization, or of assuming that India is at the origin of Mayan culture. I am merely trying to be objective.

Accordingly, shouldn't we, in the light of the above, compare Mayan society to a deck of cards, which is itself an expression of some kind of fourfold division? Each of the four suits of thirteen cards, from the ace to the king, may perhaps be said to represent a line of descendants; and by the same token, each color may possibly be looked upon as the determinant of one's place in a directed world. The temptation is great. . . . All the more so since all of this can be perfectly adapted to the fifty-two-year Mayan cycle with its four cardinal points.

The Mayans believed that the fifty-two-year cycle was based on the image of man. Therefore, from the standpoint of society, the world and its organization should logically reign on a higher level. In the calendrical system, the level is fixed at the very top—in other words, it is multiplied by twenty. In the schools for priests, the young novitiates were probably taught that since man was represented by a period of fifty-two years, society was represented by: 52 times 20 = 1,040 years.

Is it possible to uncover the traces of this higher organization?

At one point, Landa observed that the Mayans of Yucatán knew about the Sacred Round Calendar of 260 days but that they had lost sight of the principle that enabled them to compute time from the beginning of a determinate chronological moment—a moment that their Petén cousins had invented. The Indians of the peninsula were satisfied to utilize only part of the "Long Count." The mechanism for this part of the system was called the "katun wheel." Landa has thoroughly described its function.

As already indicated, in the vigesimal system each line or row had a name of its own and the transition to a higher line required the multiplication of any given figure by twenty. In the second row, however, the multiplier was not twenty but eighteen. As you will remember, this was a device to make the solar year of 365 days come out right—that is, to make it arrive at the correct total: tun. In other words, 18 times 20 = 360 days. The reader will recall the meaning of tun: the arithmetical year that was used to avoid confusion.

On the top line, the multiplier reverted to the figure twenty. This line, or katun, therefore ran as follows: 360 times 20 = 7,200 days.

To avoid confusion about the number of days, I must remind the reader that the katun consisted of twenty tun.

In choosing the katun as the basic unit of the calendar, the Indians of Yucatán were aware that the last day of each katun, that is, the Sacred Round Calendar day *ahau,* was thirteen successive times preceded by a different number. In the thirteen ensuing katuns, the same series of numbers again appeared on the last day. This is how the series went:

13 ahau, 11 ahau, 9 ahau, 7 ahau, 5 ahau, 3 ahau, 1 ahau, 12 ahau, 10 ahau, 8 ahau, 6 ahau, 4 ahau, 2 ahau, and then the cycle began all over again with 13 ahau, 11 ahau, 9 ahau, etc. These thirteen katuns, which Landa called the katun wheel, constituted the following slice of time:

13 times 20 = 260 tun (or arithmetical years).

In order to fix a katun within this slice of time, one has only to indicate the last day of a katun, preceded by its number. Actually, the number itself will suffice because it always refers to only day, ahau. The books of Chilam-Balam are a good example. Whenever the author wishes to indicate a date, he says: "In the beginning of katun 8," "at the end of katun 6" or "in the middle of katun 7" such and such an event took place. Events are therefore fixed with more or less precision within a period of 260 arithmetical years. For a modern historian, the problem is to fix these katun wheels accurately in time. If his calculation is faulty, he may make a mistake of 260 years!

The generally accepted view is that the Yucatecs calculated time in a way that oversimplified the Mayans' Long Count. Here I should like to state that I personally believe that

something entirely different is involved. In my opinion, the
katun wheel basically reflects the fourfold division at the top
level. The 1,040 years that comprise the four parts were
probably distributed—like the 52-year cycle—among the four
cardinal points. Consequently, each corner of the world contained:

1,040 divided by 4 = 260 years, or one katun wheel.

If my assumption is correct and if such a system did indeed
exist, it should be possible to find some trace of it. Once again,
Landa, in his *Relación de las Cosas de Yucatán*, comes to my
aid by furnishing additional information. The katun, he re-
marks, was a very important entity. The elapsed-time count
was represented by a god.

When one katun came to an end, another katun, which in
turn was to last twenty years, began. Landa claims, however,
that it actually lasted only ten years—in other words, for only
half of its reign. Thereafter, it did not rule alone. An idol of
the katun that was to succeed it was placed in the sacred hut
or temple alongside the idol of the present katun. The two
idols stood side by side during the last ten years of the cycle.
The idol of the second katun also received offerings; these,
however, were not as highly prized as those presented to the
idol of the first katun. At the termination of the full twenty-
year cycle, the idol of the outgoing katun was removed from
the temple and the idol of the new katun, that had already
been in the temple for ten years, now reigned alone. When the
rule of this katun ended, its idol was removed and so it
continued. These periodic dual reigns had serious repercussions of an occult nature during the latter part of the twenty-
year cycle. The repercussions produced either good or evil
consequences, depending upon the qualities attributed to the
second katun. And these qualities, in turn, were determined
by the location of the katun at one or another of the four
traditional cardinal points.

Doesn't the same principle operate within the social organization whenever the chief of one line of descendants, whose
reign is drawing to a close, yields his position of authority to

his successor? Both men have identical titles, but the successor is descended from a line of ancestors different from that of his predecessor, a line located at a different extremity of the four cardinal points.

Stretched out on the ground here at Yaxchilán, near the entrance of the small temple, I now ask myself whether the scene on the lintel perhaps depicted some such important phase of the socio-religious life of the Mayans. The two figures facing one another are dressed in identical finery and are offering each other identical emblems. Their titles, too, are identical. They meet exactly as the ritual requires, and they are descended from different lines of ancestors. The larger of the two figures is the chief in power; the smaller figure is his successor.

This system of rotation, modeled after the fifty-two-year cycle, was admirably suited to Mayan society. It made possible a definitive but equitable division of the work required not only to erect the sacred cities but also to maintain and administer them smoothly.

Many of the written sources about the Mayans of Yucatán confirm these facts. The questionnaires addressed at the end of each katun (every twenty arithmetical years) to those about to occupy the highest posts in Mayan society were proof of the existence of the obligatory replacement of the elite at certain specified dates, determined by the quadripartite division of the world.

At the end of each katun the Mayans erected stelae on which they sculptured images of their chiefs, never of their gods. These representations were presumably images of the newly elected men, individuals deemed worthy of discharging the functions of a chief for the duration of another katun because they had succeeded in answering the famous questionnaires. Moreover, each of them was quite capable of taking this esoteric examination, having lived for ten years at the side of a chief who possessed all the necessary knowledge in view of his experience as a leader.

All this data points to the obligatory rotation of the elite, a practice modeled after the rotation of the calendars at the top level (with twenty as the unit of measure, not one). And the katun wheel is, of course, one of the four identical elements which, distributed over the four cardinal points, represented the Mayan universe.

But another unknown factor still remains: the chronological point of departure that is called baktun 13. Specialists in the field concede that they do not know why the Mayans chose to make that date a milestone in their history.

For months and months I have tried to understand the reason for this choice. Other experts have worked persistently to solve the problem. Here, in the solitude of Yaxchilán, I am obsessed with a whole series of questions, ideas, facts. I try to introduce a bit of order into all this chaos. I keep giving up and coming back to it. I take notes and make computations. Suddenly I feel sure I have hit upon the answer.

In the vigesimal notational system, one baktun stands for four hundred tun, or arithmetical years.

Can it be that the date of baktun 13 constitutes the logical continuation of the union of the number thirteen with the vigesimal system adopted to compute time? Does it mark the boundary of the Mayans' "organized" time? If so, we would have the following formula:

13 kin   (the day) retains its value of 13.

13 uinal   = 13 times 20 = 260 days = 1 Sacred Round Calendar.

13 tun   = 13 times 18 times 20 (360) = 13 tun = 4,680 days = 18 Sacred Round Calendars.

13 katun = 13 times 20 tun (or 7,200 days) = 260 tun = 93,600 days = 360 Sacred Round Calendars.

13 baktun = 13 times 400 tun (144,000 days) = 5,200 tun = 1,872,000 days = 7,200 Sacred Round Calendars.

Thus, the Mayans believed that they were living in a temporal universe whose exact limit they had assessed: 5,200 years.

Well, I've finally crossed that Rubicon! But I'm afraid that I shall not be able to advance any farther along that calendrical path unless I discover the meaning and origin of the mysterious figure thirteen.

XVII

Venus, Key to All
the Mysteries

A SERPENT-GOD on a stone altar is staring at me with its cold, domineering eyes. From the bas-relief it seems to be defying me to answer the questions its presence poses. How can an explanation of the exchange of rites or the knowledge of the fourfold division of the universe come to my assistance? Serpent-god, your constant presence on the iconography of this civilization also requires an explanation.

In the Dresden Codex, the end of the world is depicted by a serpent pouring a stream of water earthward from its jaws. Among the Aztecs, the "Sun of Stone" is encircled by two serpents. Inside the stone all the numbers, all the days and months of the fifty-two years, are sculptured. These two examples, to name only a few among thousands of others, illustrate the close relationship that existed between time and the symbol of the serpent. What exactly is the nature of these relationships? So far no one has been able to determine this. I doubt that I shall be able to do so. So many unknown factors in the Mayan world remain, so many obscure aspects of their numbers and calendars!

The famous number thirteen, to begin with. Also the number five, a disturbing, poorly defined element, but one that is of major importance. It is an awe-inspiring element from the point of view of magical power. We can see, in the 365-day solar calendar an example of the fear it engendered. This solar year, or Calendar Round, consisted of eighteen months of twenty days each, as I have stated, plus an additional nineteenth month, *Uayeb* ("bed of the year"). This month contained five days—"the nameless days" that must never be mentioned. On these days, which were considered extremely unfavorable, no one left his house, no one washed or combed his hair. J. E. Thompson believes that the word uayeb comes from a word meaning "poisoned."

In mythology, the figure five was a symbol of bad luck. The Mayans believed that they lived in the fourth world, or in the fourth sun, the sun of the "Veritable Men." The three preceding worlds had all disappeared in some kind of cataclysm— deluge, rain of fire, etc. This fourth world was unfortunately their last one; it too would end in catastrophe, thus yielding place to a fifth world which would signal the definitive end of mankind.

In spite of the great care taken to avoid it, the number five necessarily appeared in certain rituals. Its official place in the traditional division of the universe was in the center. Even today in certain rites of Mayan-speaking Indians this figure survives in the same central position. Both ethnography and my own eyes can confirm this. In Yucatán, when the *chac*, the gods of rain, are beseeched to send their benevolent showers down to earth, the *x'men* places on the four corners of his altar table that symbolizes the world, four calabash gourds filled with baltse. This is for the four chacs at the cardinal points. The *x'men* also places a gourd in the center of the altar table. Very embarrassed by its presence, he claims that it is destined for an unnamed fifth chac who symbolizes the present. "He is the smallest but the most powerful," the sorcerer adds, "and also the most dangerous."

The American anthropologist, Robert Redfield, reported

from Yucatán that the Indians of the village of Chamkon believe in four protective spirits, the *balam,* residing in the four cardinal points whence they protect the corn fields against wild beasts or malevolent winds. There is also a fifth balam called *thup,* the "little one"; more important than the others, its place is in the center of the group. Similarly, the *cenote,* a natural spring well without which there would be no life in this waterless region, is also in the center of the village universe, between the four cardinal points. Here, we recognize the ambiguity of Indian thought: the cenote is a source of life, but it is also very dangerous, from a magical point of view. It is responsible for all the catastrophes that descend upon men because it is in the center, like the fifth magical point of the universe. The inhabitants of Chamkon compare the fifth balam to the thumb of one's hand, also called thup. You can easily hide it with your other fingers; although small, it is also highly essential.

The sporadic appearance of a fifth pole in the fourfold universe calls to mind the famous sovereign in India who rules over the four kings of the cardinal points. He does not always appear but he is there. He's exactly like the joker in our deck of fifty-two cards. It, too, rarely appears, but it exists.

Let us now attempt to interpret these notions about the number five. Five is rarely mentioned but it exists. It occupies a place in the center and manifests itself in the form of symbols that are smaller than the others but more powerful. In short, it is most mysterious. How does it appear in the calendars?

Let us take as an example the important fifty-two-year cycle (each year consisting of 365 days) and the distribution of the days throughout the four corners of the universe. At the end of this lapse of time, the solar year is thirteen days behind the regular year. Of this the Mayans were quite aware. In their quadripartite system this fifth element made up of thirteen days had to be placed somewhere. And they put it in the center whenever a leap year came around.

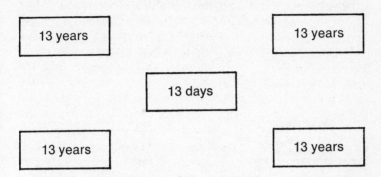

—in other words, fifty-two genuine solar years.

In starting at the very top level, the level representing the world, the Mayans got the following result:

52 times 20 = 1,040 solar years.

These solar years, dispersed to the four corners of the world, yield the following pattern:

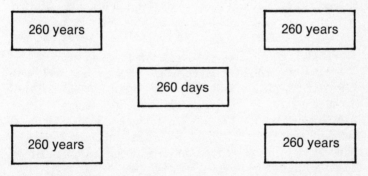

or, a total of 1,040 genuine solar years. In the elapsed-time period, 260 days were lacking, in other words, a span exactly equal to one Sacred Round Calendar year.

Thus we have a fifth element, placed in the center, smaller than the others, but highly significant since it corresponds precisely with the Sacred Round Calendar that loomed so large in the life of the Mayans.

Within this scale of time, the life of man was represented by a cycle of 52 years, whereas 1,040 years, as we have just seen, constituted the life of the world. We know that the Mayans lived in the fourth world and they awaited with great anguish the arrival of the fifth, with its final cataclysm. Their cosmic universe therefore included five worlds, or

```
+-------------------+          +-------------------------+
|    1040 years     |          |       1040 years        |
|   Second world    |          |  Third world destroyed  |
|    destroyed       |          +-------------------------+
+-------------------+
```

```
           +----------------------+
           |      1040 years      |
           |  Fifth world to come,|
           |      dangerous       |
           +----------------------+
```

```
+-------------------------+      +-------------------------+
|      1040 years          |      |      1040 years         |
|  First world destroyed  |      |  Fourth world of men    |
+-------------------------+      +-------------------------+
```

The total equals 5,200 years, or the Mayans' universe.

These 5,200 civil solar years, which we have just explained, represent the outside limit of the "organized" universe, that of the famous chronological point of departure, baktun 13.

We know that the Mayans had at their command at least two parallel systems, identical in form, and they used them to compute time in terms of the fourfold division of the universe.

Let us review the arguments once again:

ARITHMETICAL TIME

13 kin: primordial figure, which keeps the value of 13.

13 uinal: equivalent to one year of the Sacred Round Calendar of 260 days.

1 tun: distributed to the four cardinal points, 52 tun or arithmetical years.

13 katun: distributed over the four cardinal points, 1,040 tun or arithmetical years.

13 baktun: 5,200 tun, or the sum total of five worlds (one world equals 1,040 arithmetical years).

ORGANIZATION OF TIME ACCORDING TO CIVIL SOLAR YEAR

In the beginning was the figure 13, the symbol of time.

Birth of man: the union of 13 with 20, or 260 years, or the Sacred Round Calendar.

Life of man: union of the Sacred Round time and solar time, or 52 years.

Life of the world: 52 times 20 = 1,040 years.

Life of the universe: five worlds, or 1,040 times 5 = 5,200 years.

But the Mayans did not confine themselves to these two parallel systems. They created a third, endowed with great magical significance, which is called the Venus Calendar because it is based on the revolutions of Venus in the heavens.

This calendar provides us with many fascinating and precise facts about the number five and the idea of time among the Mayans.

On the basis of modern astronomical observations, we know that Venus makes a single synodical revolution—that is to say, it revolves around its initial position in the heavens within the space of 58,392 days. Each revolution of this planet is divided into four distinct periods. For eight months of the year it is the Morning Star. Then it disappears for three months. We see it again for eight months as the Evening Star. Then it vanishes again for fourteen days before reappearing as the Morning Star.

In the Dresden Codex we note with astonishment that the Mayans had codified these periods with perfect accuracy and that they had synchronized them with the lunar years.

All the measurements taken by the Indian astronomers were objective and precise. However, through direct observation we note that the revolutions of the planet Venus are irregular. This irregularity is spread out over five successive revolutions each of which comes to, respectively: 580, 587, 583, 583, and 587 days. To obtain the average number of days per Venus year, the Mayans added the five years and then divided by five. The result was 584 days—the average Venus year.

The Dresden Codex tells us more than this. Impressed by the five irregular years in the revolutions of Venus, the Mayans noted that these corresponded exactly with the eight 365-day Calendar Round years of their solar calendar. Thereupon the priest-astronomers conceived the idea of fixing an identical point of departure for both the Venus Calendar and the Calendar Round: 2,920 days—or eight solar years and five Venus Calendar years—elapsed before the first day of one calendar again coincided with the first day of the other. This was a fact so pregnant with meaning that the priest-astronomers decided to combine the two calendars in order to obtain a third calendar, whose basic unit would be the Venus-Solar year of 2,920 days.

But, while this important year was elapsing, the eight 365-day solar years that composed it were running two days behind schedule (owing to the leap years). In other words, after 130 Solar-Venus years, the 1,040 civil solar years were running a total of 260 days behind the elapsed time of the solar progression which, as we have noted, came to exactly one year of the Sacred Round Calendar. Well aware of this fact, the Mayans were astonished to note that the passage of 1,040 365-day solar years paralleled in every respect that of the Venus Calendar: there was absolutely no difference in elapsed time. The Mayans thus found themselves to be living in a bewitched time running behind solar time but yet in perfect harmony with the planet Venus. I personally am convinced that precisely here lies the key to all the enigmas of the Mayan peoples.

Let us examine the facts calmly.

Real time was determined by the progression of the synodical revolutions of Venus. Within this rigid framework, the civil solar year, or Calendar Round year, no longer required emendations because of the leap years. As a consequence, the Solar-Venus year became the true unit of time, a kind of primary and universal source of measurement, an exact landmark that would determine the progression of time and thereby systematize it accurately.

The entire pattern of cosmic time was inescapably obliged to adopt the structure of this amazing system.

In the thinking of the Mayans, the divisions of time were burdens carried by the gods at their respective stations in the four corners of the universe. A fifth station in the center would appear from time to time. Accordingly, the Solar-Venus year was divided into a) five Venus years or stations (one of the latter in each corner of the universe and a fifth in the center) and b) eight solar years or stations within this framework.

The sketch below illustrates this point.

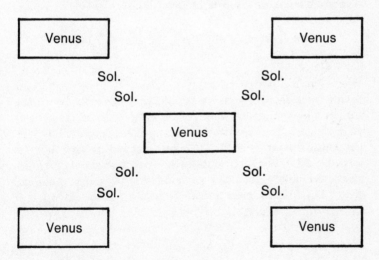

You have but to glance at it to realize that there are thirteen different stations of time. Here, then, is to be found the answer to the question about the number thirteen, foundation of all determined real time.

Once they had hit upon this pattern, the Mayan astronomers were able to understand time clearly. The leap years were absorbed into that perennially magical and dangerous area, the center. In any case, however, leap years ceased to be important because the 365-day Calendar Round cycle allowed greater precision in the measurement of real time as determined by the planet Venus.

The symbolic figure for Venus was therefore the number five. The different stages of that planet's revolutions numbered five, not four—the number that stood for the divisions of the world. And this fifth stage was placed in the center.

The priest-astronomers concentrated on searching for moments in time when the Venus Calendar coincided with the others—the Sacred Round Calendar, the Calendar Round year, the Solar-Venus year. The Dresden Codex tells us about the first union of these four calendars. Thus:

> 13 Venus-Solar years equal:
> 65 Venus years which in turn equal:
> 104 solar years and
> 146 Sacred Round Calendar years.

This was a marvelous coincidence which, no less than thirteen times in a row, dramatically placed the standard unit we have just described under the symbol thirteen. Let me elaborate: 65 years of Venus' synodical revolutions, spread over the five obligatory stations of Venus, equals 13 Venus years per station; 104 solar years, spread over eight stations, gives us 13 years for each station. To wit:

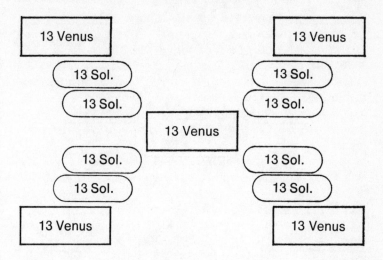

Now let us see if these meetings in time can be adapted to the previously determined arithmetical system and to the civil solar year systems.

> 104 civil solar years—65 Venus years—146 Sacred Round years—13 Venus-Solar years.
>
> 1,040 civil solar years—650 Venus years—1,460 Sacred Round years—130 Venus-Solar years.
>
> 5,200 civil solar years—3,250 Venus years—7,300 Sacred Round years—650 Venus-Solar years.

The Mayan world (1,040 civil solar years or 650 Venus years) gives us the following pattern:

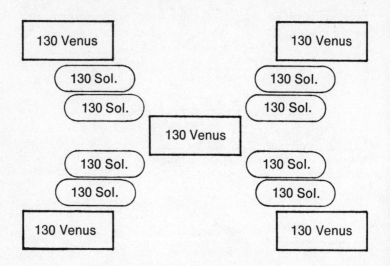

A total of 3,250 Venus years spread over the five key stations of the universe gives us five worlds of 650 Venus years each, or 1,040 solar years.

We thus have a confirmation of our system.

The cosmic vision of the Mayan universe appeared then in the form as shown on page 195.

At last I have dissected the Mayans' monstrous cosmic system! When the priest-astronomers elaborated it, they doubtless believed that they held the key to the riddle of the universe. They had the intoxicating sensation of having become the masters of the world. By imposing the laws governing time on the social organization of their people, they also made themselves the unrivalled teachers of mankind. Arithmetic, art, astronomy, writing, ceremonies and religion—all these were created and perfected for the sole purpose of serving the prescribed time pattern. By doing what they did, the priest-astronomers also strengthened the power of the elite.

Yet these master-sorcerers, rulers of both time and men,

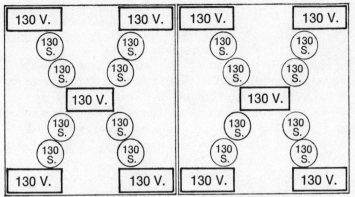

Second world **Third world**

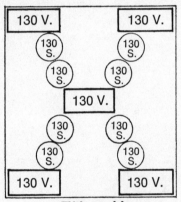

Fifth world

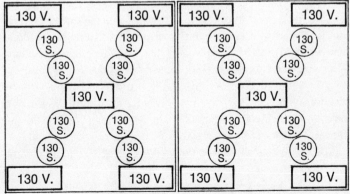

First world **Fourth world**

were the first to fall victim to this infernal system that bore within itself the seeds of its own destruction.

Let us return once more to the problem. Since each world had 1,040 years, the end of the fourth world—the world of the inventive Mayans, the Veritable Men—would come after 1,040 times 4 = 4,160 years. A total of 3,982 years stretched between the start of Mayan chronological time (baktun 13) and the latest classical date inscribed on stone. The end of the fourth world was therefore only 168 years away.

We can transpose this time into our own chronology:

The starting point of Mayan time: 3113 B.C.
The end of the fourth world: 4,160 minus 3,113 = 1047 A.D.
The date of the last classical stela: 889 A.D.
The length of time left to live before the world would end: 1,047 minus 889 = 168 years.

The imminent approach of annihilation must have filled the Mayan elite of the ninth century with a frightful feeling of anguish. Although they had not originated this devastating time system, they nonetheless believed in it even more strongly than its authors, their ancestors, had done. Each day brought them closer to the end of the world; of this they were fully and constantly aware.

The last stela erected within the framework of the fourth world cycle indicates that only thirty-eight years separated the Mayans from the final stage of 130 civil solar years. It was during this evil period that the prospect of general annihilation hung over the people like an ever-deepening shadow. Fear struck at the hearts of men. An abnormal amount of activity agitated the holy cities as the people, worried also by the imminent loss of their prosperity, grew increasingly anxious. Outside their forest lands, the northern tribes no longer needed copal or rubber for offerings to the gods.

At Xochicalco, deep in Central Mexico and some one thousand miles from Petén, a congress of astronomers met in the ninth century. Archeologists assure us that the Mayans attended this congress. They were asked to explain the solar eclipse scientifically. On the bas-reliefs of the principal temple you can still see a stone god depicted in the act of devouring the sun.

In the light of the preceding explanations, it is quite plain that this image connotes the end of the fourth world rather than a solar eclipse. The congress at Xochicalco probably represented a last desperate attempt to find some way to avert the annihilation forecast by the calendars.

The Mayans believed that only by renouncing their system of computing time could they hope to escape annihilation.

Fleeing this sacred land where they had lived for centuries and centuries, forsaking the jungle filled with their temples, palaces and corn fields, they deliberately put an end to their own world. By discarding their cosmic system, they miraculously escaped the terrible fate that was in store for them. They had to give up everything: knowledge, power, social organization, beautiful cities. It was the elite who paid the dearest price for the system they had devised. Did they simply take the road to exile and settle in another country, there to live out their lives, where time was whatever men thought it to be—the only kind of time that bore some hope of eternity?

The history of the Aztecs confirms this hypothesis. They claimed to be living in the fifth world. They feared the number four because it symbolized extinction. In their mythology, four worlds had been annihilated before their arrival on the plains of Central Mexico.

This in part explains the terror that gripped the Aztecs toward the end of each fifty-two-year cycle. Since they were living in the fifth and final world, annihilation was inevitable. Their limited cycle of time was but a reprieve. At the end of each fifty-two-year cycle they could but hope that miraculously a new cycle would begin.

All this was also true of the Indians of Yucatán, except that they had a little more time. The katun wheel constituted their measure of time, and its cycle, as we know, lasted 260 years.

Until the arrival of the Spaniards, the persistence of these calendars in Central America suggests that their originators, the great Mayans, did not disappear mysteriously after they left Petén. Determined never again to employ or even to evoke their monstrous time system upon which their entire civilization had rested, they made no attempt to live by it when they resettled elsewhere. Integrating themselves with the Mexican peoples, especially with their first cousins, the Indians of Yucatán, the members of the Mayan elite were forever content to play a self-effacing role. The only concession they did make was to communicate a few bits of knowledge to those who offered them shelter. Thanks to their hosts, we have been able to reconstitute the fabulous history of the great Mayans.

The serpent-god on the bas-relief of Yaxchilán continues to stare at me with his cold, domineering eyes. Have I answered the questionnaire correctly? Ten years—half of a katun—have elapsed since I began living in close contact with the Mayan world. The time had come to formulate a few answers.

Candelario is calling me at the top of his voice. Goodness! I had completely forgotten him. Well, let's get on. Yaxchilán is not a research laboratory, and I did not come here as a Mayan novitiate. But the hours spent here alone amid the ruins will always be unforgettable. In any case, I absolutely had to understand. . . .

I am returning to life and am happy. My companions are waiting for me on the river bank. I jump into the pirogue. What fine fishing they have had!

Kin wants to go back to his caribal. Candelario is looking forward to going down the Chixoy rapids with me. A dangerous sport, but we know we can count on each other. Besides, we both like this kind of excitement. Who knows what surprises the deserted, wild Chixoy may yet reserve for us? The demon of adventure is beckoning again. . . .

We are moving along propelled by strong strokes of the paddles. Here we come to the little beach where not long ago we ate our cooked fish with Candelario.

Without a word, Kin jumps to the ground. As far as he is concerned the entire episode of our stay is over. I watch him as he goes, his long floating tunic reaching to his ankles, his hair falling well below his shoulders. He has vanished. Already he is back in the forest world so familiar to him. This is his country. . . . Will the path he follows take him to some old temple in ruins which he alone knows, where perhaps he goes on his annual pilgrimage? Many are the Dos Pozos in these unknown lands.

A shove and we're off again in the pirogue. The Usumacinta sparkles. Today it seems to be nothing less than a royal river. A long joyous cry, loud and clear, reaches us from the distant underbrush. That's Kin saying good-bye in his own way and wishing us good luck.

Our paddles move as one. Tonight we will be far from Yaxchilán.

BIBLIOGRAPHY

DURING the past twenty years, enormous strides have been made in the domain of research on the Mayans. Monographs in English and Spanish are innumerable. I will restrict my bibliography to a brief list. Most of the books cited contain a great deal of additional bibliographical information.

The books of Chilam Balam; either the *Codice Perez* Maya-Espagnol, or the English translation by R. L. Roys (1933).

IVANOFF, PIERRE. *Cités sacrées et tribus du Mexique.* S.C.E.M.I., 1968.

LANDA, DIEGO DE. *Relación de las Cosas de Yucatán.*

MORLEY, S. G. *The Ancient Maya* (1946).

Popol Vuh. Preferably the Spanish or English translation by A. Recinos.

PROSKOURIAKOFF, TATIANA. *A Study of Classic Maya Sculpture* (1950).

———. *An Album of Maya Architecture* (1946).

SPINDEN, H. J. *Maya Art and Civilization* (1913–1957).

STEPHENS, J. L. *Incidents of Travel in Central America, Chiapas and Yucatán* (1841).

————. *Incidents of Travel in Yucatán* (1843).

STIERLIN, H. *Maya.* (1964).

TEEPLE, J. E. *Maya Astronomy* (1931).

THOMPSON, J. E. *Grandeur et décadence de la civilisation maya.* Paris: Payot, 1958.

————. *Maya Hieroglyphic Writing* (1950).

THIS BOOK WAS SET IN

CALEDONIA AND NEULAND TYPES

AND BOUND BY

AMERICAN BOOK/STRATFORD PRESS.

IT WAS PRINTED BY

HALLIDAY LITHOGRAPH CORPORATION.

TYPOGRAPHY IS BY

BARBARA COHEN.